Nailing the Interview: Tips and Techniques for Crushing Your Next Interview

AF Delk

Published by AF Delk, 2023.

While every precaution has been taken in the preparation of this book, the publisher assumes no responsibility for errors or omissions, or for damages resulting from the use of the information contained herein.

NAILING THE INTERVIEW: TIPS AND TECHNIQUES FOR CRUSHING YOUR NEXT INTERVIEW

First edition. March 28, 2023.

Copyright © 2023 AF Delk.

ISBN: 979-8215630815

Written by AF Delk.

Nailing the Interview
Tips and Techniques for Crushing Your Next Interview

by AF Delk

Dedication

To my wife Pepe, to my daughter Pipi, and my son Bobi. And to our cat Bdul.

Disclaimer

The content of the book provided by the author is for general informational purposes only. The information provided in this book is not a substitute for professional advice and should not be relied upon as such. If you have specific questions about any content in this book, you should consult a qualified professional.

While the author strives to provide accurate and up-to-date information, they make no representations or warranties of any kind, express or implied, about the completeness, accuracy, reliability, suitability, or availability of the information contained in this book for any purpose. Any reliance you place on such information is therefore strictly at your own risk.

In no event will the author, their affiliates, partners, employees, or agents be liable for any loss or damage including without limitation, indirect or consequential loss or damage, or any loss or damage whatsoever arising from loss of data or profits arising out of, or in connection with, the use of the content provided in this book.

Through this book, you may be able to link to other websites or sources that are not under the control of the author. The author has no control over the nature, content, and availability of those sources. The inclusion of any links does not necessarily imply a recommendation or endorse the views expressed within them.

Every effort is made to keep the content of this book accurate and up-to-date. However, the author takes no responsibility for, and will not be liable for, the book being temporarily unavailable due to technical issues beyond their control.

By using the content provided in this book, you hereby consent to this disclaimer and agree to its terms.

Job interview

A job interview is a formal conversation between a job seeker and a representative of an organization (usually a hiring manager or HR personnel) in which the job seeker is evaluated for their suitability and qualifications for a specific job position. The purpose of a job interview is to give the organization the opportunity to learn more about the candidate's skills, experience, personality, and work style, and to assess whether they would be a good fit for the job and the company culture. The job seeker, on the other hand, has the opportunity to learn more about the job requirements, the company, and the work environment, and to demonstrate their qualifications and interest in the position.

Job interviews are needed to assess a candidate's qualifications, skills, and suitability for a specific job position. They provide employers with an opportunity to evaluate a candidate's knowledge, experience, and personality to determine if they would be a good fit for the organization and the role.

Job interviews also give candidates a chance to learn more about the job and the company they are applying to work for. During an interview, candidates can ask questions about the company culture, work environment, and job responsibilities to help them determine if the position is a good fit for their career goals and personal values.

Overall, job interviews are a crucial part of the hiring process as they help employers make informed hiring decisions and provide candidates with an opportunity to showcase their skills and experience.

Human resources (HR) professionals typically decide to interview a candidate based on several factors, including:

1. Meeting job requirements: HR will review your resume and application to see if you meet the minimum qualifications for the job. If you do, they may decide to invite you for an interview.
2. Relevant experience: If you have relevant experience in the industry or field, HR may see you as a good candidate and decide to interview you.
3. Referrals: HR may also decide to interview you if you were referred

by someone within the company or by a trusted professional in the industry.

4. Stand-out application: A well-crafted resume, compelling cover letter, and professional online presence can make you stand out from other candidates and catch the attention of HR.

5. Cultural fit: HR may be looking for candidates who not only have the necessary qualifications and experience but also fit well with the company culture and values.

Overall, HR's goal is to identify the most qualified and suitable candidate for the job, and they will use various factors to determine if you should be invited for an interview.

There are several types of interviews that employers may use during the hiring process, including:

1. Phone interviews: These are typically the first round of interviews and are used to narrow down the pool of candidates before inviting them for in-person interviews.

2. Video interviews: These are becoming more common, especially since the COVID-19 pandemic. They can be live or pre-recorded and allow employers to see and hear candidates without needing to meet in person.

3. In-person interviews: These are traditional face-to-face interviews and may take place one-on-one or with a panel of interviewers.

4. Group interviews: These involve multiple candidates being interviewed at the same time, either individually or as a group.

5. Behavioral interviews: These are structured interviews that focus on how a candidate has handled specific situations in the past. The idea is that past behavior is a good predictor of future behavior.

6. Technical interviews: These are used to assess a candidate's technical skills and may involve coding challenges, problem-solving exercises, or other technical tasks.

7. Case interviews: These are often used in consulting, finance, and other industries and involve presenting a hypothetical business scenario and asking the candidate to analyze it and offer solutions.

8. Panel interviews: These involve being interviewed by multiple interviewers at the same time, typically from different departments or levels of the organization.

A walk-in interview is a type of interview where job seekers can directly approach the employer or the recruiting company without an appointment. Typically, a walk-in interview is conducted on a specific day and time, and candidates are interviewed on a first-come, first-served basis.

Walk-in interviews are commonly used by companies to fill immediate vacancies or seasonal positions. They are usually held at the company's premises, and candidates are required to bring their resume and other necessary documents with them. In some cases, candidates may be asked to fill out an application form or complete a skills test on the spot.

During a walk-in interview, the candidate will typically meet with a recruiter or hiring manager for a brief initial interview. This interview is usually designed to assess the candidate's qualifications and determine whether they are a good fit for the company. If the candidate is successful, they may be invited back for a more detailed interview or offered the position on the spot.

Walk-in interviews can be a great opportunity for job seekers to meet with potential employers, showcase their skills and experience, and land a job quickly. However, they can also be highly competitive, and candidates will need to be well-prepared, professional, and able to make a strong impression in a short amount of time.

It's difficult to provide a specific percentage as it can vary depending on the company, the position, and the number of applicants. Generally, the acceptance rate at the interview stage may be lower than earlier stages such as the application or resume screening process. However, if you are well-prepared and confident in your abilities, you can increase your chances of being accepted. It's important to remember that the interview is just one step in the hiring process and even if you are not accepted, it doesn't necessarily mean you are not a qualified candidate.

Preparing for a job interview is important for several reasons. First and foremost, it helps you to present yourself as a qualified and capable candidate who is well-suited for the job. By preparing for the interview, you can anticipate the questions that may be asked and prepare thoughtful and well-crafted responses that highlight your skills, experience, and qualifications.

Additionally, preparing for a job interview can help to boost your confidence and reduce anxiety. When you feel prepared and knowledgeable about the position and the company, you are more likely to feel calm and composed during the interview, which can help you to perform better.

Another important reason to prepare for a job interview is that it demonstrates your interest and commitment to the position and the company. Employers want to hire candidates who are enthusiastic and invested in the job, and preparing for the interview is a great way to show that you are serious about the opportunity.

Preparing for a job interview can help you to make a positive impression and stand out from other candidates. By demonstrating your knowledge of the company, your understanding of the position, and your ability to articulate your qualifications, you can leave a lasting impression on the interviewer and increase your chances of being offered the job.

Here are some top tips for interviews:

1. Research the company: Before the interview, research the company to gain an understanding of its mission, values, culture, and products or services. This will show your interest in the company and demonstrate your knowledge of the industry.
2. Practice common interview questions: Prepare responses to common interview questions, such as "What are your strengths and weaknesses?" or "Why do you want to work for our company?" This will help you to articulate your qualifications and showcase your skills and experience.
3. Dress appropriately: Dress professionally and appropriately for the interview. This shows that you take the opportunity seriously and are respectful of the interviewer's time.
4. Be on time: Arrive on time for the interview or a few minutes early to show that you are reliable and punctual.
5. Listen carefully: Listen carefully to the interviewer's questions and answer them thoughtfully and directly. If you don't understand a question, ask for clarification.

6. Showcase your skills: Use examples from your past experience to demonstrate your skills and abilities. This can help to illustrate your qualifications and show how you could add value to the company.
7. Follow up: After the interview, follow up with a thank-you note or email to the interviewer to express your appreciation for the opportunity and reiterate your interest in the position.

By following these tips, you can increase your chances of making a positive impression on the interviewer and landing the job.

A story about how someone got their dream job despite not fulfilling the basic requirements.

Meet Emily. Emily had a passion for marketing and dreamed of working for a well-known advertising agency. However, she did not have a college degree, which was a requirement for most entry-level marketing positions. Despite this, she decided to apply for an internship at one of the top advertising agencies in her city.

During the interview, Emily demonstrated her enthusiasm for the industry and her willingness to learn. She shared her personal marketing projects, which showcased her creativity and marketing skills. Emily's interviewers were impressed by her passion and potential and decided to take a chance on her.

As an intern, Emily worked hard to prove herself and learn as much as she could. She was a quick learner and showed a natural talent for marketing. Within a few months, she was offered a full-time position at the agency, even though she still did not have a college degree.

Over the years, Emily continued to learn and grow in her role. She attended marketing conferences and training programs, and eventually became a successful marketing director at the same agency. Emily's dedication and hard work paid off, and she was able to achieve her dream job despite not meeting the basic requirements.

This story is a reminder that sometimes passion, dedication, and hard work can overcome traditional requirements for a job. By demonstrating a willingness to learn, a strong work ethic, and a genuine passion for the industry, it is possible to achieve your dream job, even if you don't fulfill all the basic requirements.

The story highlights the importance of showcasing passion, willingness to learn, and hard work during the interview process, even if you don't fulfill all of the basic requirements for the job. In Emily's case, her enthusiasm and natural talent for marketing impressed her interviewers enough to overlook the fact that she did not have a college degree, and ultimately led to her being offered an internship and later, a full-time job. The interview process can be an opportunity to showcase your strengths and potential, and demonstrate why you are the best candidate for the job, even if you don't meet all of the basic requirements on paper.

Body language is an important aspect of communication, especially during job interviews or other professional interactions. With the increasing trend of virtual interviews and remote work, body language cues may be even more important now, as they can help to convey confidence, professionalism, and engagement, even from a distance.

Here are some tips for using body language effectively during virtual interviews:

1. Sit up straight: Maintain good posture during the interview to convey confidence and professionalism.
2. Make eye contact: Look directly at the camera to make virtual eye contact with the interviewer, which can help to build rapport and demonstrate engagement.
3. Use hand gestures: Use natural hand gestures to emphasize points or convey enthusiasm, but avoid excessive movements that can be distracting.
4. Smile: A genuine smile can help to convey warmth and positive energy, which can help to build a connection with the interviewer.
5. Dress appropriately: Dress professionally for the interview, which can help to boost your confidence and convey respect for the opportunity.

By using effective body language cues during virtual interviews, you can enhance your communication skills and make a positive impression on the interviewer, even from a distance.

Research the company

Researching the company is an important step in preparing for a job interview. Here are some tips on how to research a company:

1. Visit the company's website: The company's website is a great place to start when researching the company. Check out the "About Us" section to learn about the company's mission, values, and history.
2. Look up the company on social media: Follow the company's social media accounts to get a sense of its culture and brand identity. This can also give you insights into current projects, events, and company news.
3. Check out company reviews: Websites like Glassdoor and Indeed can provide reviews and insights from current and former employees about the company culture, work-life balance, and salary expectations.
4. Research the industry: Research the industry in which the company operates to gain a broader perspective on its place within the market.
5. Look for recent news: Keep an eye out for recent news articles about the company or industry to stay up to date on any recent developments or challenges.

By conducting thorough research on the company, you can gain a better understanding of its culture, values, and goals, which can help you tailor your interview responses and demonstrate your knowledge and interest in the company.

Researching a company through a colleague can be a helpful way to gain insight into the company culture and work environment, as well as to learn more about the day-to-day responsibilities of the position you are interviewing for. If you know someone who currently works at the company you are interviewing with, consider reaching out to them for information or insights.

By researching a company through a colleague, you can gain valuable insights that may not be available through other channels, such as the company website or social media. This can help you to better understand the company culture, values, and day-to-day operations, which can help you to tailor your interview responses and demonstrate your knowledge and interest in the company.

While it's ideal to have more time to research the company before your interview, taking these quick steps can help you to gain some basic knowledge about the company that can be useful during the interview process. Remember to focus on the most important details, such as the company's mission, values, and recent news or developments.

If you are unable to find much information about the company before your interview, there are still some steps you can take to prepare:

1. Review the job description: Make sure you thoroughly understand the requirements and responsibilities of the job you are applying for.
2. Prepare some general questions: Even if you don't have specific information about the company, you can still prepare some general questions to ask during the interview. For example, you could ask about the company culture, what the day-to-day responsibilities of the job are, or what the company's goals are for the coming year.
3. Practice your interview skills: Focus on practicing your interview skills, such as answering common interview questions, highlighting your skills and experience, and demonstrating your interest in the position.
4. Be ready to adapt: Finally, be prepared to adapt your approach during the interview if you learn new information about the company or job that you weren't aware of before.

While it's always a good idea to stay positive and hopeful, prayer may not be the most effective solution for preparing for a job interview on short notice. Instead, you can try to focus on the basics of the job, your skills and experience, and your enthusiasm for the opportunity. You can also try to relax and stay calm before the interview, which can help you to think more clearly and present yourself more confidently during the interview. Remember that the interviewer is likely aware that you may not have had much time to prepare, and that they are primarily interested in learning more about your skills, experience, and interest in the job.

It's possible that a company may give you short notice for an interview to see how well you can handle pressure and adapt to unexpected situations, but it's also possible that they simply have a tight schedule and need to fill the position quickly.

While it's important to have a strong interest in the companies you apply to, it's not always necessary to only apply to companies that you absolutely love. Sometimes, the job market may be competitive or there may not be many job openings in your field, which may require you to apply to a wider range of companies.

That being said, it's important to at least have a basic understanding of the companies you apply to, including their mission, values, and culture. If you are not interested or aligned with the values of the company, it may not be a good fit for you in the long run. Additionally, it's important to consider the job requirements, compensation, and benefits offered by the company, as these are also important factors in determining whether a job is a good fit for you.

Ultimately, it's about finding the right balance between applying to companies you are truly interested in and being realistic about the job market and your job search goals. By applying to a range of companies and focusing on finding the right fit for your skills, experience, and career goals, you can increase your chances of finding a job that you enjoy and that aligns with your values.

When it comes to job searching, it's important to be both strategic and realistic. Applying to a wide range of companies can increase your chances of finding a job, especially if you are just starting out in your career or if you are looking to switch fields. However, you also want to make sure that the companies you apply to align with your career goals and values.

Here are some additional tips to consider when applying for jobs:

1. Research the companies you are interested in. This includes not just their mission and values, but also their reputation, industry trends, and any recent news or events related to the company. This can help you better understand what the company is looking for in a candidate and whether it's a good fit for you.
2. Tailor your application materials to the job and company. This includes customizing your resume and cover letter to highlight your relevant skills and experience, and using keywords and phrases that match the job description and the company's values.
3. Network with people in your field or industry. This can help you

learn about job openings and get inside information about companies you are interested in. It can also help you make connections that may lead to future job opportunities.

4. Be open to opportunities outside your comfort zone. Sometimes, the best opportunities come from unexpected places. Don't be afraid to explore jobs that may not be a perfect match on paper, but that could offer valuable experience and opportunities for growth.

By keeping these tips in mind and being strategic in your job search, you can increase your chances of finding a job that you enjoy and that aligns with your career goals and values.

If after doing research, you find that a company doesn't align with your values or career goals, then it may not be the best idea to apply to that company. However, sometimes there may be other factors to consider, such as the job responsibilities, potential for growth, or the company's culture.

In these cases, it may be worth considering applying to the company and using the interview process to learn more about the role and the company. This can help you make a more informed decision about whether the company is a good fit for you. Additionally, it's important to keep an open mind and be flexible in your job search. Sometimes, a job that initially doesn't seem like a good fit can turn out to be a great opportunity.

It's possible to feel overwhelmed when doing research on a future company, especially if you're trying to gather a lot of information in a short amount of time. However, it's important to pace yourself and break the research down into manageable tasks. Start by focusing on the most important aspects, such as the company's mission, values, and culture.

You can then move on to researching the company's products or services, their competitors, and their financial performance. You can also look into any recent news or press releases related to the company.

It's important to remember that you don't have to know everything about the company, but having a general understanding of their business can be helpful in the interview process. If you feel overwhelmed, take a break and come back to the research when you feel more refreshed. And remember, it's okay to ask questions during the interview process to fill in any gaps in your knowledge.

Companies in the same industry or field may share some similarities in terms of culture, ethics, responsibilities, and salary standards. However, there can also be significant differences between companies within the same industry.

For example, two software development companies may have similar cultures of innovation and collaboration, but one may prioritize work-life balance while the other prioritizes long hours and tight deadlines. Similarly, two hospitals may have similar ethical standards but may have different approaches to patient care and medical research.

It's important to do research on each individual company to get a sense of their specific values and practices, rather than assuming that all companies in a particular industry are the same. This can help you make more informed decisions about where you want to work and can help you tailor your job search to companies that align with your goals and values.

Companies in the same industry or field are often competitors. While they may share similarities in terms of culture, ethics, and responsibilities, they may also have differences in their business models, target markets, and strategies. Competitors may have different approaches to marketing, product development, pricing, and distribution, which can impact their overall success in the market.

Researching competitors can be helpful in understanding the broader industry landscape, identifying potential threats or opportunities, and staying up-to-date on trends and innovations. However, it's important to maintain a professional and ethical approach to gathering information about competitors and to avoid engaging in any unethical or illegal practices, such as stealing trade secrets or engaging in price-fixing.

It's generally not ethical to ask a friend who works for a competitor to share confidential or proprietary information. It's important to respect the confidentiality of your friend's employment relationship and to avoid putting them in a difficult position.

However, it may be appropriate to ask for general information about the industry or to get their perspective on trends or challenges in the market. This can help you get a broader perspective on the industry and can help you identify potential opportunities or risks.

It's also important to be transparent about your intentions and to avoid misrepresenting yourself or your organization. If you are seeking information that could be seen as confidential or sensitive, it may be better to consult with a legal or compliance expert to ensure that you are following all applicable laws and regulations.

While it's understandable that you may want to rely on a friend for information about a competitor, it's important to consider the potential risks and ethical concerns involved. Asking your friend to share confidential information about their employer could put both of you in a difficult position, and could potentially harm your friend's career or even lead to legal action.

Instead, it may be more appropriate to seek information from publicly available sources, such as industry publications or news articles, or to conduct your own research on the company's website or through other publicly available channels. This can help you gather the information you need to make informed decisions about your own career or business, while also maintaining a professional and ethical approach.

The job ad or job description should be considered as your bible because it provides a roadmap for what the employer is looking for in a candidate. By closely examining the job ad, you can gain insight into the key skills, qualifications, and experience that the employer is seeking, and tailor your application and interview responses accordingly. Here are some ways you can utilize the job ad to increase your chances of success:

1. Understand the job requirements: Look for key phrases and qualifications that are mentioned in the job ad, such as specific technical skills, years of experience, or educational requirements. This will help you understand the level of experience and expertise that is expected for the role, and ensure that you meet the minimum qualifications.

2. Tailor your resume and cover letter: Use the job ad as a guide for customizing your resume and cover letter to the specific job. Highlight your relevant experience and qualifications that match the job requirements, and use similar language and terminology to show that you understand the role.

3. Prepare for the interview: Use the job ad to anticipate the types of questions that may be asked during the interview. Think about how your experience and qualifications align with the job requirements,

and be prepared to provide specific examples of how you have demonstrated the required skills and experience.

4. Research the company: Use the job ad to learn more about the company and its culture. Look for clues in the job ad about the company's values, mission, and goals, and use this information to tailor your responses during the interview and demonstrate your fit with the company culture.

By using the job ad as your guide, you can demonstrate your understanding of the role and the company, and increase your chances of success in the application and interview process.

Mock interviews

Mock interviews are practice interviews that simulate the real job interview experience. They are usually conducted by a career coach, mentor, or friend who acts as the interviewer and provides feedback on your performance. The purpose of a mock interview is to help you prepare for the actual interview by identifying areas where you need to improve and giving you an opportunity to practice your responses to common interview questions. By conducting mock interviews, you can gain confidence, improve your communication skills, and reduce anxiety during the real interview.

Mock interviews are important for several reasons:

1. They help you practice your interview skills: Mock interviews provide an opportunity to practice answering common interview questions and get feedback on your responses. This can help you feel more prepared and confident during the actual interview.

2. They help you identify areas for improvement: A mock interview can reveal areas where you may need to improve your communication skills, body language, or tone of voice. Getting feedback on your performance can help you make necessary adjustments before the actual interview.

3. They reduce anxiety and stress: By practicing in a simulated environment, you can reduce anxiety and stress associated with the actual interview. This can help you perform better and make a positive impression on the interviewer.

4. They help you tailor your responses to the job: By reviewing the job description and conducting mock interviews, you can better understand the job requirements and tailor your responses to demonstrate how your skills and experience align with the position.

Overall, mock interviews can be a valuable tool in your job search process, helping you to improve your interview skills, build confidence, and increase your chances of success in landing your dream job.

The Most Common Questions

Here are some of the most common job interview questions that you may encounter:

1. Can you tell me about yourself?
2. What are your strengths and weaknesses?
3. Why are you interested in this position?
4. What are your long-term career goals?
5. How would you handle a difficult situation with a coworker or supervisor?
6. What motivates you in your work?
7. Can you describe a time when you had to overcome a challenge or obstacle?
8. What skills or experiences do you bring to this position?
9. Why should we hire you?
10. Do you have any questions for us?

It's important to prepare for these types of questions and have thoughtful and concise answers ready. Additionally, be prepared to answer any questions specific to the company or the position you are applying for.

While common interview questions can provide a helpful starting point for interview preparation, it's important to keep in mind that each interview and position is unique. It's a good idea to customize your interview preparation to the specific job you're applying for and the company you're interviewing with. This can involve researching the company's mission and values, reviewing the job description and requirements, and considering how your skills and experience align with what the employer is looking for. By doing so, you'll be better equipped to answer any questions that may come up during the interview and show how you can contribute to the company's success.

It is a good idea to prepare answers for the most common job interview questions. This can help you feel more confident and prepared for the interview, and it can also help you articulate your skills and experience in a clear and concise way. However, it's important to remember that your answers should be tailored to your specific experiences and the job you are interviewing for, rather than using generic or canned responses.

Preparing answers for common job interview questions is a great way to improve your chances of success in the interview. By doing so, you'll have a better idea of how to answer questions confidently and clearly. Additionally, it will allow you to think more deeply about your skills and experience, and how they relate to the job you are applying for.

When preparing your answers, it's important to keep in mind that your responses should be tailored to your specific experiences and the requirements of the job. Avoid giving generic or canned responses, as this can make you appear unprepared or insincere.

By preparing answers to these and other common interview questions, you'll be better equipped to handle the interview process and impress potential employers. Remember to be authentic, confident, and positive in your responses, and to tailor your answers to the specific needs of the job and the company you are interviewing with.

Can you tell me about yourself?

It's an open-ended question that provides you with the opportunity to introduce yourself to the interviewer, highlight your strengths, and provide a brief overview of your professional background.

When answering this question, it's important to focus on the relevant aspects of your professional experience and background. You can start with a brief summary of your education, previous work experience, and any relevant skills or certifications you possess. You should also highlight any achievements or accomplishments that are relevant to the position you're applying for.

It's also important to tailor your response to the specific job you're applying for. This means highlighting aspects of your experience and background that are most relevant to the position, and demonstrating how you are uniquely qualified for the job.

Overall, the "Tell me about yourself" question is an opportunity to make a positive first impression and set the tone for the rest of the interview. By preparing a thoughtful and tailored response, you can demonstrate your qualifications and show the interviewer that you are a strong candidate for the position.

When an interviewer asks you to tell them about yourself, it's best to focus on professional aspects rather than personal details. You can mention your education, work experience, skills, accomplishments, and career goals. It's also okay to briefly touch on hobbies or interests that are relevant to the job or demonstrate relevant skills, such as leadership or teamwork.

However, it's generally best to avoid personal details such as your family life, religion, or political beliefs unless they are directly relevant to the job or the company's culture. Remember that the interviewer is looking to assess your professional fit for the position, not your personal life.

It's generally best to follow the lead of the interviewer and not offer personal details unless specifically asked. If an interviewer does ask about personal details, it's okay to answer. Sharing some personal details can help break the ice and create a more comfortable and personable environment during the interview. However, it's important to remember to keep it professional and relevant to the job or the company culture. You can talk briefly about your hobbies or interests that are related to the job or the industry, but avoid sharing personal information that is not relevant or may be considered inappropriate. It's also important to focus on how your personal qualities and experiences make you a good fit for the position.

Here are some samples of how to answer this question:

1. Hi, my name is [Name] and I am a fresh graduate with a degree in [Field]. During my studies, I interned at [Company] where I gained hands-on experience in [Skills]. I am passionate about [Field] and I am excited to bring my skills and enthusiasm to a new role.

2. I have been working as a [Position] for [Company] for the past [Number of Years]. In my role, I have developed expertise in [Skills] and have led successful projects such as [Project Name]. I am now looking for new challenges and opportunities to further develop my skills.

3. My background is in [Field] and I have been working in the industry for over [Number of Years]. I am passionate about [Field] and have developed a strong understanding of [Skills]. I am now looking for a new role where I can use my expertise to contribute to a dynamic team.

The key to answering this question is to keep your response concise, relevant, and focused on your professional experience and goals. You can highlight your education, relevant work experience, and key skills or strengths that make you a good fit for the position. It's also important to tailor your response to the specific job you are applying for and highlight how your experience and skills align with the requirements of the role.

A fresh graduate can definitely get opportunities for interviews. While some companies may require prior work experience, there are many entry-level positions that are open to recent graduates. It's important for a fresh graduate to highlight their academic achievements, internships, and any relevant extracurricular activities to demonstrate their skills and qualifications. Additionally, networking and attending job fairs can help increase the chances of landing an interview.

For a fresh graduate, it is common to not have any prior work experience, especially if they have just completed their studies. However, they can highlight any relevant experience they might have gained through internships, volunteer work, or extracurricular activities.

For example, if a fresh graduate has completed an internship in a relevant field, they can talk about the skills they learned and the projects they worked on during the internship. Similarly, if they have volunteered in an organization, they can talk about the responsibilities they had and the impact they made. They can also highlight any leadership roles they might have had in extracurricular activities, such as leading a team or organizing an event.

In addition to highlighting their experience, a fresh graduate can also talk about their academic achievements, such as any awards, scholarships, or research projects they might have undertaken. They can also discuss their career goals and how they see themselves contributing to the organization they are interviewing for.

It is important for a fresh graduate to demonstrate their eagerness to learn and grow in their career, as well as their willingness to take on new challenges and responsibilities. This can help them stand out in a competitive job market and increase their chances of being selected for an interview.

Organizational experience can be an important factor in the hiring decision for a fresh graduate. While a candidate may not have any professional experience, they may have had internships, volunteer work, or extracurricular activities that demonstrate relevant skills and competencies.

Employers may also look for transferable skills, such as communication, problem-solving, and time management, that a candidate has developed through their organizational experiences. These skills can be applied to various roles and industries and can be just as valuable as technical skills.

Overall, while organizational experience may not be as extensive as professional experience, it can still play a significant role in demonstrating a candidate's potential and fit for the role.

Having relevant certificates can play a significant role in getting accepted for a job interview, especially in technical or specialized fields. Certificates demonstrate that you have the necessary skills and knowledge to perform the job tasks effectively. It shows that you are willing to put in the effort to develop your skills and are committed to your professional development. Having certifications in your field can also set you apart from other candidates who may not have the same level of expertise.

Aside from education and any relevant certifications, there are several other items that a fresh graduate may want to highlight during an interview:

1. Relevant coursework or projects: Fresh graduates may not have work experience, but they can still showcase their skills and knowledge by discussing relevant coursework or projects completed during their studies.
2. Internships or volunteer work: Any relevant internships or volunteer work can demonstrate practical experience and a willingness to learn.
3. Extracurricular activities: Being involved in extracurricular activities, such as clubs or sports teams, can demonstrate teamwork and leadership skills.
4. Soft skills: Fresh graduates can highlight their soft skills, such as communication, problem-solving, and time management, which can be just as important as technical skills.

It's true that fresh graduates may be more manageable and easier to train, which can make them attractive to some employers. However, it's important for them to showcase their strengths and potential during the interview process.

Fresh graduates may have less work experience and may be willing to accept a lower salary compared to more experienced candidates. This can make them attractive to some employers, especially those who are looking to save costs or who are willing to invest in training and development for their employees. However, it's important for fresh graduates to know their worth and not undervalue themselves in the job market.

What are your strengths and weaknesses?

"What are your strengths and weaknesses?" It's a way for the interviewer to get to know you better and to see if your strengths align with the requirements of the job, and if your weaknesses can be worked on or are not deal-breakers.

When answering this question, it's important to be honest but also strategic. Focus on your strengths and highlight how they can contribute to the company and the job you are applying for. Provide examples of how you have demonstrated these strengths in the past.

For weaknesses, it's important to show self-awareness and a willingness to improve. Avoid using clichés such as "I'm a perfectionist" or "I work too hard." Instead, think of a genuine weakness that you have recognized and provide an example of how you are actively working on improving it.

For example, you could say, "One weakness I've identified is my lack of experience in project management. However, I have been taking online courses to develop my skills in this area, and I'm eager to apply what I've learned in a real-world setting."

Overall, the key is to be authentic and demonstrate a willingness to learn and grow.

The question "What's your biggest weakness?" can be one of the most challenging questions to answer in a job interview. However, with the right strategy, you can turn this question into an opportunity to showcase your self-awareness, willingness to learn, and ability to overcome challenges. Here are some tips for answering this question:

1. Be honest but strategic: You want to be truthful about your weaknesses, but also make sure that you choose a weakness that is not a critical aspect of the job you're applying for. You don't want to raise red flags or give the impression that you're not qualified for the position. For example, if you're applying for a job that requires strong communication skills, don't say that your weakness is public speaking.

2. Show self-awareness: Demonstrate that you have a clear understanding of your weaknesses and how they affect your work. You can talk about how you've struggled with this weakness in the

past and what steps you've taken to address it. This shows that you have self-awareness and are committed to personal growth.

3. Share a plan for improvement: After discussing your weakness, share a plan for how you are working to overcome it. This could include steps you're taking to improve your skills, seeking feedback from colleagues or mentors, or taking classes or training.

4. Emphasize your strengths: After discussing your weakness, make sure to emphasize your strengths and how they make you a strong candidate for the position. You want to end on a positive note and remind the interviewer of why you're a good fit for the job.

The key to answering the "What's your biggest weakness?" question is to show that you have self-awareness, a willingness to learn and grow, and the ability to turn weaknesses into strengths.

If you are unsure about your strengths and weaknesses, it can be helpful to take some time for self-reflection and assessment. Here are some tips to help you:

1. Ask for feedback: Ask colleagues, friends, or family members about what they think your strengths and weaknesses are.

Feedback can be subjective or objective, depending on how it is given and received. Subjective feedback is based on personal opinions, feelings, and perceptions, while objective feedback is based on measurable data, facts, and observations.

Both types of feedback can be valuable, depending on the context and the purpose of the feedback. Subjective feedback can provide insight into how someone is perceived by others and can help identify areas for improvement in interpersonal skills or communication. Objective feedback can provide specific information about performance metrics and can help individuals identify areas for improvement in specific tasks or skills.

Ideally, feedback should be a combination of both subjective and objective elements, providing both personal insights and specific data to help individuals improve their performance. The key is to ensure that feedback is constructive and delivered in a supportive manner, focusing on areas for improvement rather than criticism or blame.

Objective feedback is based on observable, measurable, and factual information. It is unbiased and focuses on specific behaviors or outcomes. For example, objective feedback might include statements such as "You completed the project on time," or "Your presentation was well-organized and engaging."

Subjective feedback, on the other hand, is based on personal opinions, interpretations, and perceptions. It is often influenced by individual biases, emotions, and experiences. Subjective feedback might include statements such as "I didn't like the way you presented the information," or "You need to improve your communication skills."

It's important to note that feedback can often contain elements of both objectivity and subjectivity. However, it's important for feedback to be as objective as possible in order to be fair and useful for the recipient.

1. Assess your past experiences: Think about situations where you excelled and situations where you struggled. What were the factors that contributed to your success or failure?

When assessing past experiences, it's important to focus on the skills and knowledge gained from those experiences rather than dwelling on any negative aspects of past employers or situations. Objectively, you can reflect on your past experiences by reviewing your job responsibilities, achievements, and challenges you faced.

Consider how your past experiences have helped you develop skills and knowledge that are relevant to the job you're applying for. Also, think about any areas where you may have room for improvement and how you can work on developing those skills.

Assessing your past experiences objectively involves looking at what you accomplished in your previous roles, the challenges you faced, and how you overcame them. You should also consider what skills you developed in those roles and how they could be relevant to the position you're applying for.

It's important to be honest with yourself about why you left previous companies or positions. If there were challenges or issues that you struggled with, consider how you could improve in those areas in the future. You can also consider reaching out to former colleagues or managers to ask for feedback on your performance and areas for improvement.

If you left a company on bad terms, it can be difficult to assess your experience objectively. However, it's still important to try to identify any skills or accomplishments that you gained while in that role, as they can still be valuable in future positions. It's also important to be transparent about your reasons for leaving the company, while focusing on the positive aspects of your experience.

Overall, assessing your past experiences objectively involves looking at the facts of what you accomplished and learned, while being honest with yourself about any challenges or issues that may have arisen.

1. Take a personality or strengths assessment: There are many online assessments available that can help you identify your strengths and weaknesses. Examples include the Myers-Briggs Type Indicator and the CliftonStrengths assessment.

The Myers-Briggs Type Indicator (MBTI) is a personality assessment tool that was developed by Katherine Briggs and her daughter Isabel Myers based on the theories of Carl Jung. The MBTI assesses an individual's personality across four dichotomies: extraversion vs. introversion, sensing vs. intuition, thinking vs. feeling, and judging vs. perceiving. The resulting personality type is a combination of four letters, such as ISTJ or ENFP, that describes an individual's preferred ways of thinking, feeling, and behaving. The MBTI is often used in career counseling and development to help individuals understand their own strengths and weaknesses, and to help them find career paths that are well-suited to their personality types. However, it's worth noting that the MBTI has been subject to criticism and controversy, and some experts argue that it may not be a reliable or valid measure of personality.

The Myers-Briggs Type Indicator (MBTI) is a personality assessment tool that can be useful in a variety of ways. Here are a few examples:

- Understanding your own strengths and weaknesses: The MBTI can help you understand your natural preferences and tendencies, which can give you insights into your strengths and areas for development.
- Career development: By identifying your personality type, you can gain a better understanding of the types of jobs and work environments that might be a good fit for you.
- Team building: The MBTI can be used to help build stronger teams by identifying individual strengths and preferences and how they can complement each other.
- Communication: The MBTI can provide insights into how different people communicate and process information, which can be useful in improving communication and reducing misunderstandings.

Overall, the MBTI can be a valuable tool for self-awareness, personal growth, and improving interpersonal relationships.

The CliftonStrengths assessment is a popular personal assessment tool designed to help individuals identify their top talents or strengths. The assessment is based on the concept that people perform better and are happier when they focus on their strengths, rather than trying to fix their weaknesses.

The assessment consists of 177 questions, which are designed to identify the individual's top five strengths out of a list of 34 talent themes. The themes range from Achiever, Analytical, and Adaptability to Empathy, Harmony, and Strategic.

The assessment was developed by the Gallup organization and is widely used by individuals, organizations, and coaches to help people understand their unique strengths and how to apply them in their personal and professional lives.

The CliftonStrengths assessment and the Myers-Briggs Type Indicator (MBTI) are both tools designed to help individuals better understand themselves and their personal strengths. However, there are some differences between the two.

The CliftonStrengths assessment focuses specifically on identifying an individual's top five strengths, out of a possible 34 themes. It is intended to help individuals identify and leverage their natural talents and abilities in order to achieve greater success in their personal and professional lives.

The CliftonStrengths assessment categorizes 34 themes, each representing a specific talent or quality. The top five strengths for an individual depend on their specific results. However, here are the 34 themes in alphabetical order:

- Achiever
- Activator
- Adaptability
- Analytical

- Arranger
- Belief
- Command
- Communication
- Competition
- Connectedness
- Consistency
- Context
- Deliberative
- Developer
- Discipline
- Empathy
- Focus
- Futuristic
- Harmony
- Ideation
- Includer
- Individualization
- Input
- Intellection
- Learner
- Maximizer
- Positivity
- Relator
- Responsibility
- Restorative
- Self-Assurance
- Significance
- Strategic
- Woo. WOO is one of the 34 themes or strengths identified by the CliftonStrengths assessment. It stands for "Winning Others Over" and refers to a person's ability to engage and persuade others, as well as their natural charm and social skills. People with a high WOO strength are often outgoing and energetic, and they enjoy meeting new people and making connections. They are often skilled at

networking and can be effective in sales, marketing, and other roles that require strong interpersonal skills.

In contrast, the MBTI is a personality assessment that aims to identify an individual's innate preferences across four different dichotomies: extraversion/introversion, sensing/intuition, thinking/feeling, and judging/perceiving. It is often used to help individuals better understand their communication and learning styles, as well as their strengths and potential areas for growth.

1. Reflect on your values and goals: Consider what is most important to you and what you want to achieve in your career. This can help you identify areas where you excel and areas where you may need to improve.

Your values are the principles and beliefs that are most important to you, such as honesty, integrity, compassion, or creativity. Your goals are the objectives that you want to achieve in your career, such as advancing to a leadership role, contributing to a meaningful project, or working for a specific company.

By identifying your values and goals, you can gain insight into the types of work environments and tasks that will be most fulfilling for you. For example, if you value creativity and innovation, you may be most satisfied working in a dynamic and fast-paced industry like technology or media. If your goal is to contribute to a greater cause, you may be interested in pursuing a career in non-profit or social impact work.

Reflecting on your values and goals can also help you identify areas where you may need to improve. For example, if one of your values is collaboration, but you struggle to work effectively in teams, you may need to develop your communication and interpersonal skills.

Overall, taking the time to reflect on your values and goals can help you align your strengths and weaknesses with your career aspirations, and identify opportunities for growth and development.

By taking the time to assess your strengths and weaknesses, you will be better prepared to answer this common interview question and also have a better understanding of your own skills and abilities.

Why are you interested in this position?

A common interview question that helps employer understands your motivations and interests. Your response to this question should demonstrate that you have researched the company and the position, and that you have a genuine interest in working for the organization.

When answering this question, you should highlight how your skills and experiences align with the requirements of the position. It is also important to discuss how the company's mission, values, and culture align with your own personal and professional goals.

To prepare for this question, you should research the company and the position to understand their mission, values, and culture. You should also review the job description to identify the key responsibilities and requirements of the position. Based on this information, you can craft a response that highlights your interest in the position and your alignment with the company's goals and values.

While salary and benefits are important factors in considering a job offer, it may not be the best idea to mention money as the main motive for your interest in the position during a job interview. Instead, you can focus on the skills and experience you hope to gain from the role, how it aligns with your career goals, and the potential for growth and development within the company. You can also highlight your passion for the industry or the company's mission and values as reasons for your interest in the position.

While it is true that many people work to earn money, stating it as the primary reason for being interested in a position during an interview might not come across as professional or the best way to present yourself to a potential employer. Employers typically want to hear that you are interested in the position because of the job itself, the company culture, or the opportunities for growth and development. These reasons show that you are motivated by more than just money and that you are genuinely interested in the job and the company. It is important to strike a balance between honesty and professionalism in your response.

Being an ideal candidate does not necessarily mean that you are not being honest. It is possible to be both honest and an ideal candidate. However, it is important to remember that being an ideal candidate involves more than just being honest. It also means that you have the necessary skills, qualifications, and experience for the position, as well as a good attitude, strong work ethic, and a passion for the work. While honesty is certainly an important value, it is just one of many factors that employers consider when evaluating candidates.

While salary is certainly an important factor for many people when considering a job, it is not the only factor. Other factors such as job satisfaction, work-life balance, growth opportunities, company culture, and job responsibilities can also play a significant role in job satisfaction and overall career success. So while money is important, it may not be the only or even the most important factor for everyone.

It's generally best to discuss salary and benefits during the negotiation stage, after you have been offered the job. That way, you have more leverage to negotiate and can ensure that the offer aligns with your expectations and the value you will bring to the company. However, it's important to research typical salary ranges for the position beforehand so you have an idea of what to expect and what is reasonable to negotiate for.

Negotiating salary and benefits is a separate topic from discussing your interest in the position during the interview. It's important to focus on demonstrating your qualifications and fit for the role during the interview, and then you can address salary and benefits once a job offer is extended.

Here are some examples of how you might answer the question "Why are you interested in this position?" in a more detailed and persuasive way:

Example 1: "I am very interested in this position because it aligns with my career goals and offers the opportunity to apply my skills and experience in a meaningful way. I am particularly drawn to this company because of its reputation for innovation and its commitment to making a positive impact on society. In addition, I have been following the company's recent projects and I am impressed by the level of teamwork and collaboration that goes into each one. I believe that my experience working on cross-functional teams and my passion for the industry make me an excellent fit for this role."

Example 2: "I am excited about this position because it represents a chance for me to further develop my skills and gain experience in an area that I am very passionate about. I have been following this company for some time now and I am impressed by the innovative solutions that it provides to its clients.

As someone who is always looking for new challenges, I believe that this role will allow me to expand my knowledge and take on new responsibilities. In addition, I appreciate the company's focus on professional development and its commitment to providing its employees with opportunities to learn and grow."

Example 3: "I am very excited about the opportunity to work in this position because it aligns with my career goals and interests. I have always been passionate about [specific industry or field], and this role will allow me to use my skills and experience to make a meaningful contribution to the company. Additionally, I am impressed by the company's commitment to [specific company value or mission statement], and I would be proud to be a part of such a dedicated team."

Example 4: "I am interested in this position because I believe that I have the necessary skills and experience to excel in this role. As someone who has worked in [specific job function or industry], I have a deep understanding of the challenges and opportunities that come with this type of work. I am excited about the prospect of working on [specific project or task that is relevant to the position], and I believe that my experience in [specific skill or expertise] will be an asset to the team. I also appreciate that this company values [specific company value or mission statement], and I look forward to contributing to that culture."

Example 5: "I am very interested in this position because I have been following the company's work for some time and have been impressed by its impact on [specific industry or issue]. I believe that this role would be an excellent opportunity for me to contribute to that work and to learn from some of the best in the business. Specifically, I am excited about [specific aspect of the job, such as working with a particular team or using a specific skill], and I believe that I would be a good fit for the role because of my [specific experience or qualities]."

It's important to tailor your answer to the specific position and company you are applying for. Do your research ahead of time and identify the key aspects of the job that align with your skills and interests, and be prepared to articulate those in your answer.

It's not a good idea to share personal financial hardships or other issues during a job interview. Instead, focus on your qualifications, skills, and experiences that make you a strong fit for the position and the company. You can express your enthusiasm and passion for the job without divulging personal details or coming across as desperate. Remember to remain professional and keep the conversation focused on the job and the company.

While it's understandable to feel desperate when job searching, it's not advisable to express that desperation in an interview. It's important to present yourself as a qualified and motivated candidate, rather than someone who is solely in it for the money or out of desperation. Instead of focusing on personal financial struggles, you could focus on your qualifications and interest in the company or industry. For example:

"I'm very interested in this position because it aligns perfectly with my career goals and past experience. I'm excited about the opportunity to use my skills and knowledge to contribute to the success of the company. I've done my research on the company and I'm impressed with its reputation for innovation and dedication to its customers. I believe that my qualifications and passion for this industry make me a strong candidate for this position."

In general, it's not recommended to bring up personal financial difficulties during a job interview, regardless of the industry. Doing so can give the impression that you are solely interested in the job for financial reasons, rather than being genuinely interested in the company and the work that they do. It's important to focus on your qualifications, skills, and experiences that make you a good fit for the position, and why you are interested in the opportunity.

That being said, if you are asked a specific question about your motivation for seeking the position, it's okay to briefly mention that you are looking for stable employment and career growth opportunities. However, it's important to avoid coming across as desperate or overly focused on money. Instead, focus on your passion for the industry and your desire to contribute your skills and expertise to the company.

What are your long-term career goals?

It's important to provide a thoughtful and well-crafted response to this question as it can give the interviewer insight into your career aspirations and how the position you are applying for fits into your long-term goals. Some tips for answering this question include:

1. Be honest: Don't try to give a generic answer that you think the interviewer wants to hear. Be truthful about your career goals and what you hope to achieve.
2. Be specific: Provide details about what you hope to achieve in your career and how you plan to get there. This will show that you have thought about your long-term goals and have a plan in place to achieve them.
3. Make it relevant: Connect your long-term career goals to the position you are applying for. Show how the position can help you develop the skills and experience you need to achieve your goals.
4. Be flexible: While it's important to have long-term career goals, it's also important to be flexible and open to new opportunities that may come your way. Show that you are open to different career paths and willing to adapt as needed.

Here are some examples of strong responses to the question, "What are your long-term career goals?"

1. "My long-term career goal is to continue growing in my field and eventually reach a leadership position where I can use my skills and experience to make a positive impact on my team and the company as a whole."
2. "I am passionate about personal and professional development, and my long-term career goal is to become an expert in my field while continuously learning and taking on new challenges."
3. "My ultimate goal is to contribute to a company's success and growth over the long-term. I am looking for a position that will allow me to

develop new skills and gain valuable experience, so that I can eventually take on more responsibilities and contribute even more to the organization."

4. "My long-term career goal is to find a role that aligns with my personal values and allows me to make a meaningful impact on the world. I believe that with hard work and dedication, I can achieve this goal and make a real difference in my chosen field."

Remember, it's important to be authentic and honest in your response while also demonstrating how your long-term goals align with the company and position you are applying for.

It is possible for someone from the company to sense if a candidate has an ulterior motive during an interview. Recruiters and hiring managers are often experienced in reading between the lines and picking up on nonverbal cues that may indicate dishonesty or insincerity. It is important to be honest and transparent during the interview process, as it is a chance for both the candidate and the company to assess whether they are a good fit for each other. It is also important to remember that the company is looking for someone who is not only qualified for the position but also a good cultural fit for the organization. Candidates who are open and genuine in their communication are more likely to make a positive impression on the interviewer and be considered for the position.

It's difficult to say for sure if someone from the company can sense your true motives during an interview, as it depends on various factors such as the interviewer's level of experience and intuition, as well as how well you are able to hide your true intentions.

However, there may be some signs that could suggest the interviewer is picking up on your motives. For example, if they seem hesitant to discuss certain aspects of the job or the company, or if they ask follow-up questions that seem to probe deeper into your reasons for wanting the job, it could indicate that they are sensing some ulterior motives.

Ultimately, it's important to be honest and transparent in your job search, as it will help you find a job that is a good fit for you and your goals in the long run. If you are not interested in a job for the right reasons, it's better to decline the offer and continue your job search elsewhere.

Being honest during an interview is important, but there are limitations to what you should share. You should be truthful and accurate in your responses to interview questions, but avoid oversharing personal information or negative opinions about previous employers.

Instead, focus on highlighting your skills, accomplishments, and experiences that relate to the position you are interviewing for. Be transparent about your qualifications, but don't volunteer information that is not relevant to the job.

If you are asked about a challenging situation or a negative experience, be honest but tactful. Emphasize what you learned from the experience and how it helped you grow as a professional. Remember, the goal is to present yourself in the best possible light while remaining authentic and truthful.

How would you handle a difficult situation with a coworker or supervisor?

This question is commonly asked in job interviews to assess the candidate's ability to handle conflicts and communicate effectively in the workplace.

When answering this question, it's important to focus on how you would handle the situation in a professional and constructive manner. Here are some tips for answering this question:

1. Begin by acknowledging the situation: Start by acknowledging the difficulty of the situation and the impact it has on your work and your team. This shows that you are aware of the issue and are taking it seriously.
2. Describe your approach to resolving the issue: Explain your approach to resolving the issue, which should involve a combination of active listening, empathy, and clear communication. You can also mention any previous experience you have had in resolving similar conflicts.
3. Highlight your problem-solving skills: Emphasize your ability to analyze the situation and identify the root cause of the conflict. This can demonstrate your problem-solving skills and your ability to find solutions that benefit everyone involved.
4. Discuss the outcome: End your response by discussing the positive outcome of the situation. This shows that you are focused on finding solutions and working collaboratively to achieve your goals.

Overall, when answering this question, it's important to demonstrate your ability to handle difficult situations in a professional and constructive manner.

"Can you handle working under pressure?" is a common question asked by interviewers. The question is intended to gauge how well a candidate performs in stressful situations and how they manage their workload and time when faced with tight deadlines or unexpected challenges.

To answer this question, it's important to provide specific examples of times when you have worked under pressure in the past and how you handled the situation. It's also helpful to talk about any strategies you use to manage stress and how you prioritize tasks to ensure that deadlines are met.

Remember, it's important to be honest about your abilities and not to overstate your capacity to handle pressure. If you do not work well under pressure, it's better to be upfront about it and discuss any strategies or support you use to manage stress in the workplace.

While handling difficult situations and working under pressure may share some similarities, they are not exactly the same. Handling difficult situations with a coworker or supervisor may require conflict resolution skills, communication skills, and problem-solving skills, whereas working under pressure may require stress management skills, time management skills, and the ability to prioritize tasks effectively. However, both situations require the ability to stay calm and focused while dealing with challenging circumstances.

It's normal to have days where work can feel overwhelming or challenging. However, if you find yourself feeling constantly depressed or unhappy in your work, it may be worth considering if there are any changes you can make to improve your situation. This could include talking to your supervisor about your workload, seeking support from colleagues or a therapist, or exploring other career opportunities that align better with your interests and values.

It's important to find ways to overcome the feeling of depression at work. Here are some tips that may help:

1. Identify the cause: Try to pinpoint what is causing your depression at work. Is it your workload, difficult colleagues or something else? Once you have identified the root cause, it will be easier to take steps to address it.

2. Seek support: Reach out to colleagues, friends or family members who you can talk to about your feelings. Sometimes, just sharing your concerns can help you feel better.

3. Take breaks: Taking regular breaks throughout the day can help you recharge and feel less overwhelmed.

4. Practice self-care: Make sure you are taking care of yourself by getting enough sleep, exercise, and healthy food.

5. Seek professional help: If your depression is severe or persistent, it may be helpful to speak with a mental health professional.

Remember, it's important to prioritize your mental health and well-being, both at work and outside of work.

It is important to answer honestly during a job interview, but it is also important to frame your response in a positive light. Instead of saying that you cannot work under difficult situations or work under pressure, you could focus on how you approach these situations. For example, you could say that you recognize the importance of working effectively under pressure and have developed strategies to manage stress and maintain productivity in high-pressure situations. This shows that you are self-aware and proactive in managing your work environment, which can be a positive attribute to potential employers.

Here are some possible answers:

1. "I have found that I work best under a bit of pressure, as it helps me stay focused and motivated. However, I also make sure to take breaks and prioritize self-care to prevent burnout."

2. "I have had some experiences where I felt overwhelmed with the amount of work and pressure, but I learned that it's important to communicate with my supervisor and ask for help or additional resources when needed. I also try to stay organized and prioritize tasks to make sure I am meeting deadlines and managing my workload effectively."

3. "I think everyone has their limits when it comes to working under pressure, but I believe that I am able to handle stressful situations by taking a step back, assessing the situation and coming up with a plan to tackle it. I also make sure to communicate with my team and ask for help if needed."

4. "I've struggled in the past with working under pressure, but I recognize that it's an important skill in any job. I'm actively working on improving my ability to handle difficult situations and have been seeking out resources, such as time management techniques and stress-reduction strategies, to help me manage my workload more effectively."

Admitting to a weakness can make an interviewer question your ability to perform the job successfully. However, it is important to remember that everyone has weaknesses and it is better to acknowledge them and show a willingness to work on them rather than pretend they don't exist. It's all about framing your weaknesses in a positive light and showing that you are aware of them and actively trying to improve upon them.

What motivates you in your work?

Motivation is a key factor that drives individuals to achieve their goals and aspirations. For many people, work is an essential part of life, and being motivated in one's job can lead to personal and professional success. In this essay, I will discuss what motivates me in my work and how these motivations have shaped my career goals and aspirations.

One of the primary factors that motivate me in my work is the desire to make a positive impact on the world around me. I have always been passionate about helping others, and I believe that working in a field that allows me to make a difference in people's lives is incredibly rewarding. Whether it is through developing innovative technologies, creating new products and services, or improving existing systems, I am driven by the opportunity to make a positive impact on society.

Another factor that motivates me in my work is the opportunity for personal and professional growth. I believe that continuous learning is essential for success in any career, and I am constantly seeking new opportunities to expand my knowledge and skills. This could include attending training sessions, conferences, or pursuing advanced degrees. By investing in my personal and professional growth, I am better equipped to tackle new challenges and take on new responsibilities in my career.

Working with a team of like-minded individuals is another significant motivator for me. I find that collaborating with others who share my goals and values not only helps me to achieve more but also makes the work itself more enjoyable. When working with a team, each member brings their unique set of skills and experiences to the table, resulting in a diverse and dynamic working environment.

Finally, I am motivated by the sense of accomplishment that comes with completing a challenging task or project. Whether it is achieving a personal goal or contributing to a larger organizational objective, the feeling of accomplishment and recognition for a job well done is incredibly rewarding. This recognition can come from both colleagues and superiors and can be a powerful motivator for future success.

In conclusion, what motivates me in my work is the desire to make a positive impact on the world, personal and professional growth, working with like-minded individuals, and the sense of accomplishment that comes with completing a challenging task or project. By understanding these motivations, I am better equipped to pursue my career goals and aspirations and achieve personal and professional success.

That could be a potential answer to the interview question. The length of the answer would depend on the interviewer's expectations and the context of the interview. It's important to tailor your response to the specific job and company you're applying to and to be genuine in your answer.

Another sample answer:

What motivates me in my work is the opportunity to make a positive impact on others. As a healthcare professional, I have the privilege of helping people every day, whether it's through providing medical care, emotional support, or simply a listening ear. Knowing that I can make a difference in someone's life is incredibly rewarding and gives me a sense of purpose in my work.

Additionally, I am motivated by the challenge of constantly learning and growing in my field. Healthcare is a rapidly evolving industry, and there is always new research, technologies, and best practices to stay up-to-date on. I am driven to continuously improve my skills and knowledge so that I can provide the best possible care to my patients.

Finally, I am motivated by the relationships I build with my coworkers and colleagues. Collaboration and teamwork are essential in healthcare, and I enjoy working with others towards a common goal. Building strong relationships with my colleagues not only makes work more enjoyable, but also improves patient outcomes through better communication and coordination of care.

Can you describe a time when you had to overcome a challenge or obstacle?

The interviewer may ask this question to evaluate the candidate's problem-solving skills, resilience, ability to work under pressure, and their approach to handling challenges. By asking about a specific example from the candidate's past experiences, the interviewer can also gain insight into how the candidate approaches challenges and what their decision-making process looks like. Additionally, the question allows the candidate to showcase their accomplishments and demonstrate their ability to overcome difficult situations, which can be important in determining their suitability for the job.

Here's a sample answer to this question:

There was a time in my previous job where our team was tasked with completing a project with a very tight deadline. We were already behind schedule and the pressure was mounting as the deadline approached. To make things worse, a key team member suddenly had to take a leave of absence due to personal reasons.

As the team lead, I had to come up with a plan to ensure we still met the deadline. I had to quickly assess the situation and identify the most critical tasks that needed to be completed in order to move the project forward. I worked closely with the remaining team members to re-assign responsibilities and prioritize our work.

One of the biggest challenges we faced was that we were short-staffed and had to take on additional work without sacrificing quality. To address this, I worked closely with the remaining team members to ensure that they had the resources and support they needed to be successful. I also reached out to other departments within the company to see if we could get additional resources to help us complete the project.

Despite the challenges we faced, we were able to complete the project on time and with high quality. Looking back, I realize that this experience taught me the importance of remaining calm under pressure, being resourceful, and collaborating effectively with my team.

Overall, this experience helped me grow as a leader and gave me the confidence to tackle future challenges head-on. I believe that my ability to overcome obstacles and find creative solutions to complex problems is one of my greatest strengths, and I am eager to bring this skill set to new challenges in my career.

Another sample:

One time I had to overcome a challenge was during a major project at my previous job. I was tasked with leading a team of individuals with diverse backgrounds and skillsets to complete the project within a tight deadline. However, one of the team members was consistently missing deadlines and not contributing as much as the others.

To address the issue, I scheduled a meeting with the team member to discuss their performance and understand any potential issues that might be causing their lack of productivity. Through the conversation, I discovered that the team member was feeling overwhelmed by their workload and unsure of how to approach certain aspects of the project.

To help alleviate the situation, I worked with the team member to create a plan for prioritizing their tasks and provided additional resources to help them better understand the project requirements. I also checked in with them regularly to ensure they were making progress and offered support and guidance where needed.

As a result of our efforts, the team member was able to complete their assigned tasks on time and contribute more effectively to the project. The project was ultimately completed within the deadline and received positive feedback from the client.

This experience taught me the importance of effective communication, active listening, and problem-solving in leadership roles. It also reinforced my belief in the value of teamwork and collaboration in achieving common goals.

What skills or experiences do you bring to this position?

When an interviewer asks, "What skills or experiences do you bring to this position?" they are seeking to understand what specific abilities and qualifications you possess that make you a good fit for the job. It's an opportunity for you to highlight your strengths and unique qualities that set you apart from other candidates.

When answering this question, it's important to review the job description and requirements to identify the specific skills and experiences that the employer is looking for. Then, you can tailor your answer to highlight your strengths in those areas.

One effective way to answer this question is to use the STAR method: Situation, Task, Action, Result. This involves describing a specific situation or task you faced in a previous job, the action you took to address it, and the positive result that came from your efforts.

For example, you might say:

"In my previous job as a marketing manager, I was responsible for launching a new product line. One of the biggest challenges I faced was limited resources and a tight deadline. To overcome this, I collaborated with cross-functional teams to streamline our processes and prioritize our efforts. I also developed a targeted marketing campaign that effectively reached our target audience, resulting in a 20% increase in sales within the first quarter. Through this experience, I honed my project management and communication skills, which I believe will be valuable in this position."

In addition to highlighting specific experiences, it's also important to showcase your transferable skills, such as problem-solving, leadership, teamwork, and adaptability. Be sure to provide concrete examples that demonstrate how you have successfully utilized these skills in the past.

Overall, when answering the question, "What skills or experiences do you bring to this position?" it's important to focus on the specific qualifications and requirements of the job, and highlight your strengths and unique qualities that make you a good fit for the role.

Here are some more sample responses to the question:

1. In my previous role, I gained a lot of experience in project management and collaboration. I believe these skills would be very valuable in this position, as it involves working with a team to complete projects and meet deadlines. Additionally, I have experience with data analysis and reporting, which I think would be useful in this position for making data-driven decisions and tracking progress.

2. One of my strengths is my attention to detail, which has been honed through my experience in quality assurance roles. I have experience in developing and implementing quality control processes, as well as conducting audits to identify areas for improvement. I believe this

experience would be beneficial in this position, which requires ensuring that work is completed accurately and efficiently.

3. As a marketing professional, I have experience in developing and executing marketing campaigns across multiple channels. I am well-versed in social media marketing, email marketing, and content marketing, which I believe would be valuable in this position. Additionally, I have experience in conducting market research and analyzing data to inform marketing strategies.

4. In my previous role as a software engineer, I gained experience in coding and software development. I have a strong understanding of programming languages such as Java and Python, as well as experience with database design and development. I believe this technical expertise would be valuable in this position, which involves developing and maintaining software applications.

5. As a customer service representative, I gained experience in handling customer inquiries and resolving issues in a timely and effective manner. I am skilled in active listening, problem-solving, and conflict resolution. I believe these skills would be valuable in this position, which involves interacting with clients and providing high-quality customer service.

It's important to strike a balance when answering questions about skills and experiences that you bring to a position. While you want to highlight your strengths and accomplishments, you also want to avoid coming across as arrogant or overly ambitious. It's best to focus on your relevant skills and experiences and how they align with the requirements of the position, rather than simply trying to impress the interviewer with your achievements. You can also talk about how you plan to continue developing your skills and how you see yourself contributing to the company in the long term.

It is possible to become bored or disengaged during a lengthy interview, and this can inadvertently show in our body language, tone of voice, or the content of our responses. It's important to stay focused and engaged throughout the interview, even if it feels lengthy or repetitive.

To combat boredom, you can try to actively listen to the interviewer's questions and provide thoughtful responses, ask questions that show your interest in the company or position, or use techniques such as taking notes or repeating the question back to the interviewer to help stay engaged. Additionally, it may be helpful to prepare for the interview ahead of time by researching the company and the position, and practicing your responses to common interview questions.

If during an interview, the interviewers are talking to each other and seem to be ignoring you, it can be frustrating and make you feel uneasy. However, it's important to keep in mind that this behavior may not necessarily be a reflection of your performance or qualifications.

It's possible that the interviewers are discussing something related to the position or the company, and it may not directly involve you. Alternatively, they may be trying to gauge your reaction to the situation to see how you handle pressure or difficult situations.

In any case, it's important to remain calm and engaged during the interview. Don't let your frustration or anxiety show, as this could negatively impact your chances of being offered the job. Instead, try to maintain eye contact and actively listen to what is being said, even if it seems like the conversation isn't directed at you.

If you feel like you're being ignored or left out of the conversation, you can politely interject and ask if there's anything else you can provide or if there are any additional questions they have for you. This shows that you're engaged and interested in the position, and it can also help steer the conversation back to your qualifications and experience.

The interviewer may never come up that day, even we both side confirmed the schedule. I can understand how frustrating that experience must have been for you. It's important to remember that not all interviewers or companies will behave in such a disrespectful manner. However, if you encounter a similar situation in the future, it's important to remain professional and polite. You could send an email or make a call to follow up on the missed interview, but it's ultimately up to you to decide if you want to continue pursuing that job opportunity. It's also a good idea to research the company and read reviews from other employees or applicants before applying for a job to get a better sense of the company culture and how they treat their employees.

That experience may leave a negative impression of the company or the interviewer. It can reflect poorly on their professionalism and communication skills, which may make you hesitant to pursue any future opportunities with them. It's important to remember that interviews are not only a chance for the company to evaluate you, but also for you to evaluate the company and determine if it's a good fit for you.

Why should we hire you?

The question is a common one in job interviews, and it can be difficult to answer. However, it's an opportunity to showcase your skills, experience, and passion for the job. Here are some key points to keep in mind when answering this question:

1. Highlight your relevant skills and experience: When answering this question, it's important to focus on the skills and experience that make you a strong fit for the position. Take a look at the job description and highlight the key qualifications that the employer is looking for. Then, emphasize how your skills and experience match those qualifications.

2. Emphasize your enthusiasm for the position: Employers want to hire someone who is genuinely interested in the job and the company. Make sure to express your enthusiasm and passion for the role, and explain why you're excited about the opportunity to work for this particular organization.

3. Demonstrate your value: Employers want to hire someone who will add value to their organization. Provide specific examples of how you have added value in previous roles, and explain how you would do the same in this new position. This could include examples of how you have increased efficiency, improved processes, or contributed to the bottom line.

4. Be confident, but not arrogant: When answering this question, it's important to strike the right balance between confidence and humility. You want to showcase your strengths and achievements, but you don't want to come across as arrogant or boastful. Make sure to use specific examples and focus on how you can add value to the organization.

5. Focus on what the employer needs: Ultimately, the key to answering this question is to focus on what the employer needs. Make sure to tailor your answer to the specific requirements of the job and the company, and explain how you can help the organization achieve its

goals.

Here's an example answer:

"I believe that I would be an excellent fit for this position for several reasons. First, I have extensive experience in the field of marketing, and I am highly skilled in developing and implementing effective marketing campaigns. I have a proven track record of increasing brand awareness and driving sales, and I am confident that I could do the same for your organization.

In addition, I am incredibly passionate about the work that your company does, and I am excited about the opportunity to contribute to your mission. I believe that my skills and experience would be a valuable asset to your team, and I am committed to helping you achieve your goals.

Finally, I am confident that my strong work ethic, attention to detail, and ability to work collaboratively with others would make me a valuable member of your team. I am excited about the opportunity to work for your organization, and I believe that I would be a great fit for the role."

Here are a few more samples for the question:

1. I believe I would be an excellent fit for this position because of my combination of skills and experience. I have a strong track record of success in similar roles, and I am confident that I could make a significant contribution to your team. I am a quick learner, a strong communicator, and I have a great attention to detail. I am also passionate about this industry and I am excited about the opportunity to work with such a dynamic and innovative company like yours.

2. You should hire me because I am a highly motivated individual who is eager to learn and grow in my career. I am confident that I would bring a positive attitude, strong work ethic, and a commitment to excellence to your team. I am also a creative problem solver who is able to think outside the box and come up with innovative solutions to complex challenges. With my combination of skills and experience, I am confident that I could make a valuable contribution to your organization.

3. I believe that I am the best candidate for this position because I have

the right combination of skills, experience, and passion for the work. I have a proven track record of success in similar roles, and I am confident that I could excel in this position. I have a strong work ethic, excellent communication skills, and I am committed to delivering high-quality work on time and on budget. Additionally, I am highly adaptable and able to work well under pressure, making me an excellent fit for your fast-paced and dynamic organization.

4. I am confident that I am the ideal candidate for this position because of my extensive experience in the industry, my strong technical skills, and my ability to work well with others. I have a track record of success in similar roles, and I am confident that I could hit the ground running and make a significant contribution to your team from day one. I am also a natural problem solver who is able to work well under pressure and come up with innovative solutions to complex challenges. I believe that my combination of skills, experience, and passion for the work would make me an excellent fit for your organization.

It is important to promote yourself and your abilities while answering this question. You should highlight your relevant skills, experiences, and accomplishments that make you the best fit for the job. However, it is also important to strike a balance and not come across as too boastful or arrogant. You want to demonstrate confidence in your abilities without turning off the interviewer.

Do you have any questions for us?

The question is a common one asked towards the end of an interview. This gives you an opportunity to demonstrate your interest in the position and the company, as well as gather important information to help you make an informed decision if you receive an offer.

It's important to prepare some thoughtful questions in advance, rather than asking generic or superficial questions. Your questions should demonstrate that you have researched the company and the position, and that you are genuinely interested in learning more.

Some examples of good questions to ask might include:

1. Can you describe a typical day or week in this position?
2. What are some of the biggest challenges facing this team or department?
3. Can you tell me about the company culture and what it's like to work here?
4. How does the company support employee development and growth?
5. What qualities or skills do you think are essential for success in this role?

Asking thoughtful questions can not only provide valuable information, but also demonstrate your enthusiasm and engagement with the hiring process. It can also help you better understand whether the company and position align with your values, goals, and career aspirations.

While the question "Do you have any questions for us?" may not have a direct impact on the hiring decision, it is still an important opportunity for you to gather more information about the company, the role, and the expectations. It also shows the interviewer that you are interested and engaged in the position.

Asking thoughtful and relevant questions can also help you gain a better understanding of the company culture, opportunities for growth, and any potential challenges you may face in the role. This information can help you make an informed decision if you are offered the job. Additionally, it can also give you a chance to impress the interviewer with your curiosity, enthusiasm, and preparedness.

Asking if you have any questions for the interviewer is not just a formality. It is an opportunity for you to clarify any doubts you may have about the company or the position, and also to show that you have done your research and are genuinely interested in the job. It also gives you a chance to learn more about the company culture, expectations, and future opportunities. Additionally, the questions you ask can provide insight into your level of engagement, critical thinking skills, and fit for the position. Therefore, it is important to prepare thoughtful questions to ask during the interview.

The reality of working in a company can be different from what was presented in the interview process. However, asking questions during the interview can help you gather more information about the company, the role, and the work culture, which can help you make a more informed decision about whether the job is a good fit for you. Additionally, asking questions can demonstrate your interest in the company and the position, which can leave a positive impression on the interviewer.

The person conducting the interview may not be the direct supervisor or even have a good understanding of the day-to-day responsibilities of the position. In this case, the questions and answers may be more general and less specific to the actual job duties. However, it's still important to ask thoughtful questions that demonstrate your interest in the company and the role. Even if the interviewer cannot answer your question directly, they may be able to direct you to someone who can provide more information.

It is appropriate to ask the interviewer any questions you may have about the company, the position, or the work culture. This not only shows your interest in the company but also gives you more insight into what it might be like to work there. It is important to ask thoughtful and relevant questions that demonstrate your research and understanding of the company and the industry.

It is possible that the interviewer may provide a biased or overly positive response to your question, as they are representing the company and want to present it in a positive light. However, it is also important to note that the interviewer's response can still provide valuable insights into the company culture and work environment.

To mitigate this potential bias, you can try to ask specific and targeted questions that may give you more concrete and objective information. You can also research the company beforehand and gather information from other sources, such as employee reviews or news articles, to gain a more comprehensive understanding of the company.

It is important to remember that the interview process is not only for the employer to assess your fit for the company, but also for you to assess whether the company aligns with your values and goals. Don't be afraid to ask questions that are important to you, and use the information you gather to make an informed decision about whether the company is the right fit for you.

While insider information can be useful, it's important to be respectful and mindful of any legal or ethical considerations. It's best to avoid asking for confidential or sensitive information during an interview, as it could create an uncomfortable or awkward situation for the interviewer. Instead, focus on asking questions that will help you gain a better understanding of the company's culture, values, and work environment, as well as the role you are applying for.

Asking questions at the end of the interview may not be a key factor in determining whether you get the job or not, but it can leave a positive impression on the interviewer and demonstrate your interest in the company and the position. It can also help you gather more information about the role and the company culture to make an informed decision if you receive a job offer. So while it may not be the deciding factor, it is still an important part of the interview process.

So, what makes interviewers tick and use it to our advantage?

Understanding what interviewers are looking for can help you tailor your responses to their expectations and increase your chances of success. Here are a few things that interviewers typically look for:

1. Relevant skills and experience: Interviewers want to make sure that you have the skills and experience necessary to perform the job effectively.
2. Cultural fit: Interviewers want to know that you will fit in with the company's culture and work well with the team.
3. Enthusiasm and motivation: Interviewers want to see that you are excited about the job and motivated to succeed.
4. Problem-solving ability: Interviewers want to know that you can handle challenges and solve problems effectively.
5. Strong communication skills: Interviewers want to see that you can communicate clearly and effectively with colleagues and clients.

To use this information to your advantage, make sure you emphasize your relevant skills and experience, demonstrate your enthusiasm and motivation for the job, provide examples of your problem-solving ability and communication skills, and research the company's culture to ensure a good fit. Additionally, it's important to remain professional, engaged, and personable throughout the interview process to make a positive impression on the interviewer.

Here are some tips on how to make interviewers "tick" and use it to your advantage:

1. Research the company and the position: Before the interview, do some research on the company and the position you are applying for. This will give you a better understanding of what the interviewer is looking for and what the company values.
2. Practice your answers: Practice your answers to common interview questions. This will help you feel more confident and prepared during

the interview.

3. Show enthusiasm: Show enthusiasm for the position and the company. This can be demonstrated through your body language, tone of voice, and the way you talk about your past experiences.

4. Be prepared with questions: Have some questions prepared to ask the interviewer. This shows that you are interested in the position and the company and can help you stand out from other candidates.

5. Focus on your strengths: During the interview, focus on your strengths and how they relate to the position. This will help you demonstrate why you are the best candidate for the job.

6. Be authentic: Be yourself during the interview. Interviewers can often tell if someone is being disingenuous or not being true to themselves. Being authentic can help build rapport and create a positive connection with the interviewer.

7. Follow up: After the interview, follow up with a thank-you email or note. This shows that you are still interested in the position and can help keep you top of mind for the interviewer.

Fear is just our perception

Fear is a natural emotion that all humans experience. It can be triggered by a perceived threat, danger or uncertainty. However, fear is also largely subjective and influenced by our perceptions and interpretations of events and situations.

For example, some people may have a fear of public speaking, while others may not find it scary at all. The fear response in these situations is largely influenced by how the individual perceives the situation and their ability to handle it.

In many cases, fear can hold us back from pursuing our goals and dreams. We may feel scared of failure, rejection, or even success. However, it's important to understand that fear is often based on our perceptions and beliefs, rather than actual reality.

By challenging our perceptions and beliefs, we can learn to overcome our fears and take action towards our goals. This may involve changing our self-talk, reframing our beliefs, and gradually exposing ourselves to the things we fear in a safe and controlled way.

Ultimately, fear is just one aspect of the human experience, and it's up to us to decide how much power we give it over our lives. By understanding that fear is largely based on our perceptions and beliefs, we can learn to face our fears and live more fulfilling lives.

Even if you possess the skills, knowledge, and experience needed for a particular task or situation, you may still experience fear if you are unsure about the outcome, concerned about making a mistake, or facing a challenge that is new or difficult.

Additionally, fear can be influenced by external factors such as social pressures, cultural expectations, or personal insecurities. For example, you may fear failure or rejection because of past experiences, societal norms, or your own self-doubt.

However, it's important to remember that fear is not always a negative emotion. It can be a valuable motivator that helps us to stay alert, focused, and prepared for potential challenges. By acknowledging and understanding our fears, we can learn to manage them and use them to our advantage, rather than allowing them to control us.

While interviews can be nerve-wracking, it's important not to let fear get the best of you. Being prepared, confident, and knowledgeable about the company and position can help reduce anxiety and improve your chances of success. It's important to remember that the interviewer is also human and wants to find the right candidate for the job. So, approach the interview with a positive attitude, be yourself, and showcase your skills and experiences.

Being calm can definitely help in an interview situation. It allows you to think more clearly and respond more effectively to questions. Additionally, being calm can help you to present yourself in a more confident and professional manner, which can make a positive impression on the interviewer.

Having a good mindset to have during an interview, the fear can be easy to forget that the interviewer is also a person with their own thoughts, feelings, and vulnerabilities. When we remember this, it can help us approach the interview with empathy and a sense of connection rather than just focusing on our own nerves or anxiety. It can also help us build rapport with the interviewer and make the conversation feel more like a two-way dialogue rather than a high-pressure interrogation.

Other mindset that will help a lot is "**be yourself**" is a common phrase used to encourage individuals to express their true personality and behavior without any pretense or artificiality. When it comes to job interviews, it's important to present your authentic self to the interviewer, rather than trying to be someone you're not.

Being yourself in an interview involves showcasing your unique qualities and skills while still being professional and appropriate for the setting. It means being honest about your strengths and weaknesses, and providing genuine examples of your accomplishments and experiences. It's also important to express your enthusiasm and passion for the job, as this can demonstrate your commitment and potential for success in the role.

By being yourself in an interview, you can establish a connection with the interviewer and make a lasting impression. This can help to set you apart from other candidates who may be putting on a false persona. Additionally, it can help you to feel more comfortable and confident in the interview, which can ultimately lead to a better performance and increase your chances of being hired.

Overall, being yourself in an interview is important because it allows you to present your best self, while also being true to who you are as a person. This authenticity can help you to stand out as a candidate and increase your chances of landing the job.

Another one is, **stay positive**: Even if the interview doesn't go as well as you hoped, try to stay positive and learn from the experience. Every interview is a learning opportunity, and you can always apply what you've learned to your next one.

Staying positive during an interview is important because it helps you maintain your confidence and composure, even if the interviewer asks difficult questions or makes you feel uncomfortable. It's also important to remember that not every interview will result in a job offer, and that's okay. The key is to learn from the experience and use it to improve your performance in future interviews.

Staying positive can also help you build rapport with the interviewer, as it shows that you have a can-do attitude and are able to handle challenging situations. Even if you don't have all the qualifications or experience that the job requires, a positive attitude can sometimes make up for it.

One way to stay positive during an interview is to focus on your strengths and achievements, rather than dwelling on your weaknesses or mistakes. This can help you feel more confident and in control of the conversation. Another way is to take a deep breath and remind yourself that you're prepared and capable of handling whatever comes your way.

Lastly, it's important to remember that the interview is just one step in the job search process. Even if you don't get the job, you can still use the experience to build your skills and network with others in your field. By staying positive and maintaining a growth mindset, you can turn even a less-than-successful interview into a valuable learning opportunity.

You are better than you think you are

This mindset is important because it helps you build confidence in yourself and your abilities. Many candidates may come with impressive resumes and accomplishments, which can lead to feelings of inadequacy or imposter syndrome. However, it's important to remember that you were selected for the interview for a reason, and you have unique skills and experiences that make you a valuable candidate.

By not overestimating other candidates, you can avoid the trap of comparing yourself to them and feeling inferior. Instead, focus on your own strengths and how they align with the requirements of the position.

Additionally, **by not underestimating yourself**, you can approach the interview with a sense of self-assurance and demonstrate your confidence in your abilities. This can help you to present yourself in a positive light and make a strong impression on the interviewer.

This mindset is all about self-confidence and believing in yourself. It's easy to compare yourself to others and think that they are more qualified or experienced than you, but it's important to remember that you bring unique skills and experiences to the table.

When you underestimate yourself, you may come across as insecure or unsure of your abilities during the interview. On the other hand, when you overestimate the other candidates, you may become intimidated or nervous, which can negatively affect your performance.

Instead, **focus on your strengths** and what you can bring to the position. Believe in your abilities and show confidence in your answers and demeanor during the interview. Remember that the interviewer invited you for an interview because they saw something in your application that interested them. Use this opportunity to showcase your skills and experiences and show that you are the best candidate for the job.

Overall, maintaining a balanced perspective and believing in yourself can help you to stay focused and perform your best during the interview process.

What and how to prepare

Visualization is a technique that involves creating a mental image or scenario of a desired outcome in your mind. It's often used by athletes, musicians, and other top performers to help them achieve their goals. By visualizing success, you can train your brain to focus on the positive outcomes and overcome any negative self-talk or doubts that may arise during the interview process.

To apply visualization to an interview, you can start by creating a mental image of yourself confidently answering questions, engaging with the interviewer, and presenting yourself as a strong candidate. Visualize the environment, the people in the room, and the conversation flowing smoothly.

As you visualize yourself succeeding in the interview, try to engage all your senses. Imagine the feeling of confidence in your body, the sound of your clear voice, the sight of the interviewer's impressed expression, and the smell of the air around you. The more vivid and detailed your visualization, the more effective it will be.

The idea behind visualization is that by creating a mental image of the desired outcome, you can program your mind to work towards that outcome. By doing so, you can reduce anxiety and stress during the interview and increase your chances of success.

However, it's important to remember that visualization alone won't guarantee success in an interview. It should be used as a tool to supplement your preparation and mindset. It's still essential to do your research, practice your answers, and present yourself in the best possible light during the interview.

Visualization for an interview is not exactly like a shadow fight game, but it does involve mentally preparing and envisioning success in a similar way. In shadow fighting, you mentally prepare for a physical fight by visualizing moves and strategies ahead of time. Similarly, visualization for an interview involves mentally preparing for success by envisioning yourself confidently answering questions, connecting with the interviewer, and ultimately landing the job. It's a way to train your mind and boost your confidence so that you can perform your best during the actual interview.

While visualization is not a mandatory technique for interview preparation, it can be a helpful tool for some individuals. Visualization can help you mentally prepare for the interview, increase your confidence, and improve your performance by creating a positive mindset. It allows you to mentally rehearse how you will respond to potential questions and how you will present yourself during the interview. However, visualization should not replace the other essential components of interview preparation, such as researching the company and the position, preparing answers to commonly asked questions, and practicing with a friend or family member.

Pushing your comfort zone before the interview is important because it helps you become more confident, prepared, and adaptable. By doing things that are outside of your comfort zone, you challenge yourself to learn and grow, which can help you handle unexpected situations during the interview.

One way to push your comfort zone before the interview is to practice answering interview questions with a friend or mentor. This will help you become more comfortable talking about yourself and your experiences. You can also try role-playing different scenarios that might come up during the interview, such as difficult questions or unexpected situations.

Another technique is to do mock interviews with a career coach or professional. This will give you an opportunity to practice your interview skills in a safe environment and receive feedback on your performance.

You can also attend networking events or industry conferences to meet new people and practice your communication skills. This can help you feel more comfortable engaging in conversation with strangers, which can translate to more confidence during the interview.

Finally, you can challenge yourself to take on new projects or responsibilities at work. This will help you develop new skills and become more adaptable to change, which can be a valuable asset during the interview process.

Overall, pushing your comfort zone before the interview can help you feel more prepared and confident; this can increase your chances of success.

Bring copies of your resume, a list of references, and any other documents or materials that might be relevant to the interview. Also, be prepared to answer common interview questions and provide specific examples of your skills and accomplishments.

Making a great first impression during an interview is crucial because it sets the tone for the rest of the conversation. Here are some tips to ensure that you make a positive first impression:

1. Dress appropriately: Make sure that you dress professionally and appropriately for the job you're applying for. Avoid dressing too casually or inappropriately for the job.
2. Be punctual: Arrive on time or a few minutes early for the interview. Being late can give a bad impression and create unnecessary stress.
3. Show confidence: Walk into the interview with your head held high and greet the interviewer with a smile and a firm handshake. This shows confidence and enthusiasm.
4. Be attentive: Listen carefully to the interviewer and show that you're interested in what they have to say. Avoid interrupting or speaking over them.
5. Maintain good body language: Sit up straight and make eye contact with the interviewer. Avoid slouching or fidgeting as this can convey nervousness or disinterest.
6. Use positive language: Use positive language and avoid negative comments or complaints. Focus on your strengths and achievements rather than your weaknesses.
7. Follow up: After the interview, send a thank-you note or email to the interviewer to express your gratitude for the opportunity and reiterate your interest in the position.

By following these tips, you can make a great first impression during your interview and increase your chances of getting the job.

It's important to **project the right attitude** from the start of an interview because it sets the tone for the rest of the conversation. Your attitude can be seen through your body language, tone of voice, and overall demeanor. If you come across as disinterested, unfriendly, or negative, it can be difficult to change that perception throughout the rest of the interview.

On the other hand, projecting a positive and enthusiastic attitude from the start can make a strong impression on the interviewer. It can make them more interested in what you have to say and can help build rapport between you and the interviewer. It can also make you seem more confident and capable, which can help you stand out from other candidates.

Additionally, having a positive attitude can help you stay focused and perform better throughout the interview. When you approach the interview with a can-do attitude and a willingness to learn and adapt, you're more likely to give thoughtful and well-reasoned answers to the interviewer's questions.

Some examples of the right attitudes to project during an interview include:

1. Confidence: Be confident in your skills, experience, and abilities. Speak clearly and with conviction when answering questions.
2. Enthusiasm: Show enthusiasm for the job and the company. Let the interviewer know that you are excited about the opportunity to work there.
3. Professionalism: Dress appropriately for the interview and be polite and respectful to everyone you meet. Make sure to arrive on time or a few minutes early.
4. Flexibility: Show that you are adaptable and willing to learn new things. Employers want to know that you can handle change and are open to new ideas.
5. Team player: Emphasize your ability to work well with others and contribute to a positive work environment.
6. Problem solver: Show that you are proactive in identifying and solving problems. Give examples of how you have solved problems in the past.
7. Positive attitude: Maintain a positive attitude throughout the interview, even if you encounter a difficult question or situation. A positive attitude can be contagious and leave a lasting impression on the interviewer.

Overall, projecting the right attitude from the start can set the stage for a successful interview and increase your chances of landing the job.

The STAR framework is a helpful tool for structuring your answers to behavioral interview questions that ask you to provide specific examples of past experiences. It helps you to present your response in a clear and organized manner that is easy for the interviewer to follow.

Here's a breakdown of what each part of the STAR framework entails:

- Situation: Begin by setting the context for the situation you were in.

Describe the background, the problem you were facing, and any other relevant details.

- Task: Explain what task you needed to complete or goal you were working towards within this situation.
- Action: Detail the specific actions you took to address the situation or complete the task. Be sure to emphasize your own role in the situation, and provide specific examples of the steps you took.
- Result: Share the outcome of your actions, and describe the impact your actions had on the situation or task. Be sure to highlight any specific achievements or lessons learned.

By using the STAR framework, you can ensure that your answers are well-organized, detailed, and easy to follow, which will help you to make a strong impression on the interviewer.

The STAR (Situation, Task, Action, and Result) framework is a widely used technique for answering behavioral interview questions. It is important to use this framework to avoid common mistakes such as giving vague or generic answers, not providing enough detail or focusing too much on the situation rather than the action and result.

To use the STAR technique effectively, first, describe the situation you were in, being specific about the context and any challenges you faced. Next, explain the task or goal you were working towards. Then, describe the actions you took to address the situation and achieve the task or goal. Finally, detail the result of your actions and how they impacted the situation positively.

By following the STAR framework, you can provide detailed and specific examples of your skills and experiences, demonstrating your ability to handle different situations and overcome challenges. This approach shows your ability to think critically and solve problems, which are important skills in any job. Additionally, it shows your ability to communicate effectively and present information in a clear and concise manner, which is an important trait for any employee.

The STAR framework can be used for straightforward questions as well. For example, if the interviewer asks, "What are your strengths?" you could use the STAR framework to structure your answer.

Here's an example of how you could use the STAR framework to answer this question:

Situation: In my previous job, I was responsible for managing a team of five people.

Task: One of my main tasks was to ensure that everyone on the team was working together effectively and meeting their targets.

Action: To achieve this, I implemented a weekly team meeting where we would discuss our progress, identify any issues, and brainstorm solutions. I also made sure to meet with each team member individually on a regular basis to provide feedback and support.

Result: As a result of these actions, my team was able to achieve their targets consistently and we were recognized by the company for our high performance. Additionally, team members reported feeling more engaged and motivated in their work.

Using the STAR framework can help you provide a structured and comprehensive answer that clearly demonstrates your skills and experience.

Here are some common mistakes people make during interviews:

1. Rambling or going off topic when answering questions
2. Speaking negatively about past employers or experiences
3. Failing to research the company or position before the interview
4. Forgetting to highlight specific skills or experiences that relate to the job
5. Not asking questions or showing interest in the company or position
6. Failing to listen to the interviewer or ask for clarification when needed
7. Appearing disinterested or lacking enthusiasm for the job or company
8. Not dressing appropriately for the interview
9. Failing to follow up with a thank-you note or email after the interview.

Here are some examples of how the STAR framework can be applied to these common interview questions:

Can you tell me about a time when you faced a challenge in the workplace?

Situation: Explain the situation that you faced. Task: Describe the task or goal that you needed to accomplish. Action: Outline the steps you took to overcome the challenge. Result: Explain the outcome of your actions.

What is your greatest accomplishment in your career so far?

Situation: Describe the situation that led to your accomplishment. Task: Explain the task or goal that you had to accomplish. Action: Outline the steps you took to accomplish your goal. Result: Explain the positive outcome of your actions.

Can you give an example of a time when you had to work as part of a team to complete a project?

Situation: Describe the project and the team you were a part of. Task: Explain the task or goal that your team needed to accomplish. Action: Outline the steps your team took to complete the project. Result: Explain the outcome of your team's efforts.

Tell me about a time when you had to solve a complex problem.

Situation: Describe the situation that led to the problem. Task: Explain the problem that needed to be solved. Action: Outline the steps you took to solve the problem. Result: Explain the positive outcome of your actions.

What is your experience working with customers or clients?

Situation: Describe the situation where you had to interact with customers or clients. Task: Explain the task or goal you needed to accomplish. Action: Outline the steps you took to accomplish your task. Result: Explain the positive outcome of your actions.

Can you describe a time when you had to take on a leadership role?

Situation: Describe the situation where you had to take on a leadership role. Task: Explain the task or goal that you needed to accomplish. Action: Outline the steps you took to accomplish your task. Result: Explain the positive outcome of your actions.

What motivates you in your work?

Situation: Explain the type of work environment where you feel motivated. Task: Explain the tasks that make you feel motivated. Action: Outline the steps you take to stay motivated. Result: Explain the positive outcome of your motivation.

Tell me about a time when you had to adapt to a change in the workplace.

Situation: Describe the change that occurred in your workplace. Task: Explain the task or goal that you needed to accomplish. Action: Outline the steps you took to adapt to the change. Result: Explain the positive outcome of your actions.

What is your approach to problem-solving?

Situation: Explain the situation that led to the problem. Task: Explain the problem that needed to be solved. Action: Outline the steps you took to solve the problem. Result: Explain the positive outcome of your problem-solving approach.

Behavioral questions are designed to elicit information about how you have behaved in specific situations in the past. These questions aim to predict your future behavior and performance by looking at your past behavior.

To answer behavioral questions effectively, it's important to use the STAR method, which stands for Situation, Task, Action, and Result. Here's how you can use STAR to make your answers great:

1. Situation: Start by setting the stage for the situation. Explain the context, background, and any other relevant details about the situation.
2. Task: Describe the specific task or challenge that you faced in the situation. Be clear about what you were trying to accomplish or what problem you were trying to solve.
3. Action: Explain the actions you took to address the task or challenge. Be specific about what you did, how you did it, and why you chose that approach.
4. Result: Finally, describe the results of your actions. Be clear about what happened, what you accomplished, and what you learned from the experience.

To make your answers great, you should also follow these tips:

1. Be specific: Use concrete examples and specific details to illustrate your answers.
2. Focus on your own actions: Behavioral questions are about your behavior, so make sure you're focusing on your own actions and not

those of others.

3. Be honest: It's important to be truthful in your answers. Don't exaggerate or embellish your experiences.
4. Highlight your skills and strengths: Use the STAR method to highlight your skills and strengths that are relevant to the job you're applying for.
5. Practice: Practice answering behavioral questions before your interview so you feel confident and prepared.

These also apply for situational questions. Situational questions are a type of interview question that ask you to describe how you would handle a hypothetical situation or problem. They are designed to assess your problem-solving skills and your ability to think on your feet.

Tricky questions can be very challenging to answer, as they are designed to test your ability to think on your feet and assess your problem-solving skills. These questions can come in many different forms, ranging from brain teasers and riddles to hypothetical scenarios that require you to make difficult choices.

To answer tricky questions effectively, it is important to stay calm and focused. Take a moment to gather your thoughts and try to break the question down into smaller parts. Look for clues in the question itself and try to identify what the interviewer is really looking for in your answer.

It is also important to be honest and transparent in your responses. If you don't know the answer to a question, don't try to bluff your way through it. Instead, be upfront about your lack of knowledge and demonstrate your willingness to learn and find a solution.

Remember, tricky questions are designed to test your problem-solving skills and your ability to think creatively under pressure. Stay calm, focused, and confident in your abilities, and you will be well-equipped to tackle any tricky question that comes your way.

When an interviewer asks behavioral or situational questions, they are often looking for evidence of your problem-solving abilities and your ability to learn and adapt from experiences. Therefore, what you have learned from a situation and how you plan to implement that knowledge in the future is often more important than the situation itself.

For example, if an interviewer asks you to describe a time when you faced a difficult challenge, they are not only interested in hearing about the challenge itself, but also how you approached the problem and what you learned from it. They want to see if you have the ability to analyze a situation, come up with solutions, and then reflect on how you can improve in the future.

Therefore, when answering behavioral or situational questions, it's important to focus on the lessons you learned from the situation and how you plan to apply that knowledge in the future. This shows the interviewer that you have a growth mindset and are constantly looking for ways to improve and develop your skills.

The **criticism sandwich** is a technique for giving feedback or criticism in a constructive way. It involves sandwiching the negative feedback between two positive comments. For example, if you need to mention a negative experience with a previous employer, you could say something like:

"Well, I really enjoyed working for XYZ company because they gave me a lot of opportunities to grow and develop my skills. One thing I found challenging, however, was the communication style of some of my colleagues. But overall, I learned a lot from that experience and it helped me to improve my own communication skills."

This way, you are acknowledging the negative experience while also emphasizing the positive aspects and what you learned from it. It shows that you can handle difficult situations in a mature and constructive way.

The criticism sandwich is a technique for giving feedback or criticism in a way that is constructive and balanced. It involves starting with positive feedback or praise, then providing the criticism or negative feedback, and ending with another positive statement.

For example, if an interviewer asks about a previous project you worked on and you need to mention a challenge or issue, you could use the criticism sandwich like this:

Positive statement: "Overall, the project was a great success and we were able to achieve all of our goals within the timeline and budget."

Criticism/negative feedback: "However, there was one issue that arose when we were working on the design phase that caused a delay and required some extra resources to fix."

Positive statement: "But we were able to quickly come up with a solution, and the final result was even better than we had initially planned."

By using the criticism sandwich, you are able to provide honest feedback while still maintaining a positive tone and avoiding sounding overly critical or negative.

The **interview doesn't stop the moment you leave the room** because your behavior and actions after the interview can also impact the overall impression you make on the interviewer and the hiring team. For example, sending a thank-you email or letter after the interview can demonstrate your professionalism and gratitude for the opportunity. Similarly, following up on the status of your application in a respectful and courteous manner can show your enthusiasm and interest in the position.

On the other hand, if you behave unprofessionally or disrespectfully after the interview, it can reflect poorly on you and potentially harm your chances of getting the job. For instance, sending rude or demanding emails or messages, bad-mouthing the company or the interviewer on social media, or failing to show up for a scheduled follow-up call can all leave a negative impression.

Therefore, it's important to remember that the interview process extends beyond the physical interview and to conduct yourself in a professional and courteous manner throughout the entire process.

Follow-up after an interview is important because it shows your continued interest in the position and company, and it gives you an opportunity to address any concerns or questions that may have come up during the interview. It also provides a chance to reiterate your qualifications and thank the interviewer for their time.

Here are some tips on how to do follow-up after an interview:

1. Send a thank-you email: Within 24 hours after the interview, send a brief email thanking the interviewer for their time and expressing your continued interest in the position. Use this opportunity to also reiterate your qualifications and highlight any points you may have missed during the interview.
2. Send a handwritten note: Consider sending a handwritten note in addition to the email, as this can be a nice touch and help you stand out from other candidates.

3. Follow up on any action items: If there were any action items discussed during the interview (such as sending additional materials or completing a task), make sure to follow up on them in a timely manner.
4. Be patient: After sending your follow-up, give the interviewer some time to respond. If you don't hear back within a week, consider sending a polite and brief message to check in.

It's a good practice to always follow up after an interview. It shows that you are interested in the job and appreciate the interviewer's time. Additionally, it gives you another opportunity to showcase your enthusiasm and reiterate your qualifications for the position.

Overall, following up after an interview can help you leave a positive impression and increase your chances of landing the job.

Body language can have a significant impact on how you are perceived during an interview, and one important aspect of this is the **handshake**. A firm, confident handshake is generally considered the most appropriate and professional way to greet someone in a business setting. Here are some tips on how to shake hands effectively:

1. Make eye contact: Before you extend your hand, make sure to establish eye contact with the other person. This shows that you are engaged and interested in the interaction.
2. Extend your arm: When you shake hands, extend your arm fully and offer a firm grip. Avoid a limp or weak handshake, which can be perceived as lacking confidence.
3. Shake from the elbow: Move your arm up and down from the elbow, rather than just shaking your wrist. This creates a more natural and assertive movement.
4. Release after 2-3 seconds: It's important to release the handshake after a few seconds, as holding on for too long can be awkward and uncomfortable.

In terms of common mistakes to avoid, some people may offer a limp or weak handshake, while others may be overly aggressive or squeeze too hard. It's important to find a balance that is appropriate for the situation and the other person's body language.

Remember that the handshake is just one aspect of your body language during an interview. Other things to consider include your posture, facial expressions, and overall demeanor. By paying attention to these nonverbal cues, you can project confidence, professionalism, and a positive attitude, which can all help to make a great first impression.

There is no specific meaning or significance to a particular style of handshake. However, certain styles may be more appropriate or effective in different situations. For example, a firm handshake is generally considered a sign of confidence and competence, while a limp or weak handshake may come across as unprofessional or uncertain. In any case, it's important to be aware of cultural norms and expectations regarding handshakes in different settings, as these may vary across different regions and countries.

Donald Trump is known for his unique handshake style, which has been described as aggressive and dominant. He often pulls the other person towards him while shaking their hand, and holds onto their hand for an extended period of time. This has been interpreted by some as an attempt to assert dominance and establish control in the interaction.

Trump's handshake style has been widely discussed and analyzed in the media, and has even been the subject of parody and satire. Some have criticized it as inappropriate or disrespectful, while others see it as a power move that reflects Trump's confidence and assertiveness. However, it's important to note that not everyone will respond positively to this type of handshake, and it's generally recommended to use a more traditional and neutral handshake style in professional settings.

It would not be recommended using Donald Trump's handshake style in a job interview or any professional setting. While some people may find it impressive or assertive, others may find it overly aggressive or even disrespectful. It's important to remember that job interviews are formal settings, and it's best to stick to a more traditional, professional handshake that is firm but not too forceful. Ultimately, it's important to be respectful and mindful of the other person's feelings and preferences.

Having the **right posture** during an interview is important because it can convey confidence, competence, and professionalism. Here are some tips on how to have good posture during an interview:

1. Sit up straight: Keep your back straight and shoulders relaxed, but not slouched. This helps to convey confidence and openness.
2. Keep your feet flat on the ground: Avoid crossing your legs or fidgeting with your feet. This can convey nervousness or discomfort.
3. Maintain eye contact: Look at the interviewer in the eyes while speaking. This shows that you are confident and engaged.
4. Keep your hands in your lap or on the table: Avoid crossing your arms, as this can convey defensiveness. You can use your hands to gesture or emphasize a point, but be careful not to overdo it.
5. Avoid leaning forward or backward: This can convey discomfort or aggression. Instead, try to lean slightly forward to show engagement and interest.

Overall, good posture can help you project confidence and professionalism, and make a positive impression on your interviewer.

Touching your face during an interview can send the wrong message to the interviewer. It may indicate that you are nervous, uncertain, or even disinterested. Additionally, touching your face can be seen as unprofessional and may distract the interviewer from focusing on what you are saying.

Furthermore, touching your face can transmit germs and viruses, especially in today's world where there is heightened awareness around hygiene and health. In an interview setting, it's best to keep your hands away from your face and use hand sanitizer or wash your hands before and after the interview.

Touching your face, including your nose, and scratching can be perceived as unprofessional and may distract the interviewer's attention from what you are saying. It may also create a perception that you are nervous or unprepared for the interview. It's important to maintain a confident and professional demeanor throughout the interview, and avoiding any unnecessary physical gestures that could distract from your message can help achieve that.

Overall, maintaining good posture and avoiding unnecessary movements such as touching your face can help you appear more confident, professional, and focused during an interview.

Preparing virtual interview

There are several types of virtual interviews, including:

1. Phone Interviews: These interviews are conducted over the phone and are often used as an initial screening process.
2. Video Interviews: These interviews are conducted using video conferencing software such as Zoom or Skype. They are similar to in-person interviews but take place virtually.
3. Pre-recorded Interviews: These interviews are pre-recorded and submitted by the candidate. They are often used as a first-round screening process.
4. Panel Interviews: These interviews involve multiple interviewers who participate virtually using video conferencing software.
5. Virtual Job Fairs: These events allow candidates to connect with recruiters and hiring managers from multiple companies in one virtual location.
6. Virtual Assessment Centers: These centers are designed to test a candidate's skills and abilities through a series of virtual exercises and assessments.

Preparing for a phone, Skype, Zoom or any other virtual interview is similar to preparing for an in-person interview, with some additional considerations. Here are some tips to help you prepare for a virtual interview:

1. Test your equipment: Make sure you have a good internet connection and that your camera and microphone are working properly. Test them ahead of time to avoid any technical issues during the interview.
2. Choose the right location: Find a quiet and private place where you won't be interrupted or distracted. Make sure the lighting is good and that the background is neutral and uncluttered.
3. Dress appropriately: Dress as you would for an in-person interview, even if it's a virtual one. This will help you feel more professional and confident.

4. Have your resume and notes handy: Print out a copy of your resume and any notes you've prepared about the company or position. Keep them nearby in case you need to reference them during the interview.

5. Be on time: Treat a virtual interview just as you would an in-person interview and be on time. Log in a few minutes early to make sure everything is working properly.

6. Practice with a friend: If you're not familiar with virtual interviews, practice with a friend or family member. This will help you get comfortable with the technology and prepare you for the real thing.

7. Maintain eye contact: Look into the camera instead of at the screen to maintain eye contact with the interviewer. This will help you appear more engaged and interested.

8. Speak clearly and confidently: Speak clearly and confidently, and avoid using filler words such as "um" and "like". Take your time when answering questions and try to sound natural and conversational.

9. Follow up: Follow up with a thank-you email after the interview, just as you would after an in-person interview. This will help you stand out and show your interest in the position.

If you receive an unexpected call from the company, it's important to be prepared to answer some basic questions about yourself and your experience. Here are some tips on what to do:

1. Take a deep breath and stay calm: Getting a surprise call can be nerve-wracking, but it's important to stay calm and composed.

2. Ask for more information: Ask the person on the phone who they are and what the purpose of the call is. If you're not sure if it's a legitimate call from the company, ask for a phone number you can call back to verify.

3. Be ready to talk about yourself: The caller may ask you to talk about your experience, so be ready to give a brief summary of your background and qualifications.

4. Take notes: If the caller gives you any important information, such as the name of the person who called or their contact information, be sure to write it down.

5. Follow up: If the caller asks to schedule an interview, be sure to follow up with them promptly and confirm the details.

6. Be professional: Even though the call may have come unexpectedly, it's important to be professional and courteous at all times. Thank the caller for the opportunity and express your interest in the position.

Overall, the key to handling unexpected calls is to stay calm, gather information, and be prepared to talk about yourself and your experience.

If you're having difficulty hearing or understanding the interviewer during a phone or video interview, it's important to speak up and ask for clarification. It's better to ask them to repeat themselves or to speak louder rather than guessing or giving an answer that may not be what they are looking for. You can say something like, "I'm sorry, could you please repeat that?" or "I didn't quite catch what you said, could you please speak a bit louder?" It's better to take the time to make sure you understand the question or information being conveyed than to make assumptions and potentially miss important details.

It is perfectly acceptable to politely ask the interviewer to repeat themselves or to clarify a point if you did not hear or understand something they said during a phone or video interview. In fact, it shows that you are actively engaged in the conversation and interested in what they have to say. Just be sure to phrase your request in a polite and respectful manner, such "Could you clarify what you mean by [insert term or concept here]?"

Choosing the right environment for a virtual interview is important because it can impact your performance and the interviewer's perception of you. Here are some tips for choosing the right environment for a virtual interview:

1. Choose a quiet place: Select a quiet location with no or minimal noise. If possible, use a room with a door that can be closed to avoid any disruptions or distractions.

2. Avoid public places: Avoid conducting a virtual interview in a public place such as a coffee shop or park. These places can be noisy and distracting, and you may not have the privacy you need.

3. Check your internet connection: Ensure that your internet connection is stable and strong. Test your connection beforehand and

consider using a wired connection if possible.

4. Check your lighting: Make sure you are well-lit and visible on camera. Position yourself in a well-lit area or use additional lighting if needed.

5. Dress appropriately: Dress professionally, as you would for an in-person interview.

6. Consider your background: Choose a neutral background that is not distracting or cluttered. A plain wall or a bookshelf can be a good option.

7. Minimize interruptions: Let others in your household know that you will be in an interview and ask them to avoid interrupting you. Consider turning off your phone and closing any unnecessary programs on your computer to minimize distractions.

Avoiding reading word by word in an interview is important as it can make you appear less confident and prepared. Instead, it's better to practice and memorize key points or bullet points that you want to make, and then expand on them in your own words. This approach will help you to sound more natural and engaged in the conversation, rather than just reciting prepared answers.

Overall, choosing the right environment for a virtual interview can help you to present yourself professionally and reduce distractions that could impact your performance.

Expressing gratitude and thanking the interviewer is a simple but powerful technique that can help you build rapport and leave a positive impression. It shows that you appreciate the opportunity to interview for the position and that you value the time and effort that the interviewer has invested in the process.

To use this technique, you can say something like, "Thank you for taking the time to interview me. I really appreciate the opportunity to learn more about the position and the company." You can also express gratitude at the end of the interview, saying something like, "Thank you for your time today. It was great to meet you and learn more about the company."

Remember to be genuine in your expression of gratitude and to tailor your message to the specific circumstances of the interview. By thanking the interviewer, you demonstrate professionalism, respect, and enthusiasm for the opportunity.

Salary negotiation

Salary negotiation can be a daunting task for many people, but there are some strategies that can help you handle these challenges and get the salary you deserve:

1. Research the industry standard: Before negotiating your salary, research the industry standard for the position you are applying for. This will give you a better idea of what salary range to expect and will help you make a more informed decision when it comes to negotiating your salary.
2. Know your worth: Before the negotiation, evaluate your skills, experience, and education, and be prepared to explain how they add value to the company. This will help you justify your desired salary and demonstrate why you deserve it.
3. Be confident: During the negotiation, be confident in your abilities and the value you bring to the company. Don't be afraid to ask for what you want, but also be willing to compromise and consider other factors such as benefits, bonuses, and vacation time.
4. Wait for the right moment: It's important to let the interviewer bring up the salary discussion first. Once the interviewer brings up the topic, you can begin to negotiate.
5. Practice your negotiation skills: Practice your negotiation skills with a friend or family member, or consider working with a career coach or mentor. This will help you feel more comfortable and confident during the actual negotiation.
6. Be confident and professional: Be confident in your abilities and professional in your negotiations. State your case calmly and respectfully, and be prepared to explain why you believe you deserve the salary you are asking for.
7. Consider the whole package: When negotiating your salary, consider the whole compensation package, including benefits, bonuses, vacation time, and other perks. You may be able to negotiate a better package overall, even if you are not able to get the exact salary you

were hoping for.

8. Be flexible: Be open to compromise and consider the needs of the company as well as your own. Be willing to negotiate on other aspects of the job if you are not able to get the salary you want.

9. Have a backup plan: If you are not able to negotiate the salary you want, have backup plans in place. Consider whether the job is still worth taking at a lower salary, or if you should continue to search for other opportunities.

10. Be willing to walk away: If the employer is unwilling to meet your salary expectations, be willing to walk away from the job offer. It may be difficult, but accepting a salary that is below your worth can set you back in the long run and affect your future earning potential.

Overall, salary negotiation requires preparation, confidence, and a willingness to negotiate. By doing your research, knowing your worth, and practicing your negotiation skills, you can increase your chances of getting the salary you deserve.

Having more options can give you more power in a negotiation because it gives you leverages. If you have only one option, then you have no bargaining power because you have nothing to compare it to. However, if you have multiple options, you can compare them and choose the best one. This gives you bargaining power because you can walk away from the negotiation if the terms are not favorable.

To trigger this situation, you need to have alternative job offers or opportunities in hand. Research other companies in your field that may be hiring, or try networking to find other potential job leads. You can also consider taking on freelance work or consulting gigs to diversify your income streams and give yourself more options.

When negotiating your salary, you can mention your other options as a way to demonstrate your value and the demand for your skills. However, it's important to be tactful and not overly aggressive in your negotiation tactics. You want to come across as confident and assertive, but also professional and respectful.

Typically, the employer should initiate the discussion about salary during the interview process. However, as a candidate, it is important to be prepared to discuss your salary expectations if asked. Additionally, if you have received an offer and the employer has not discussed salary, it is appropriate to initiate the discussion and negotiate for the salary you believe you deserve based on your skills, experience, and the market value for the position.

If the interviewer does not bring up the salary topic during the interview, it is appropriate to ask about it before the end of the interview. You can say something like, "I am really interested in this position, and I was hoping we could discuss the compensation for the role. Could you tell me more about the salary range for this position?"

If you are uncomfortable bringing up the topic yourself, you can wait until the interviewer brings it up. However, keep in mind that if you wait until the employer brings it up, you may not have as much time to negotiate as you would if you initiated the discussion.

There are several signs that an interviewer may give that could indicate they are open to discussing salary negotiations, including:

1. They ask about your salary expectations or current salary.
2. They ask if you have any questions about the compensation or benefits package.
3. They mention that they are willing to negotiate salary and benefits.
4. They express a strong interest in hiring you and want to ensure you are happy with the compensation package.

If you notice any of these signs, it may be a good opportunity to initiate a discussion about salary negotiations. You can start by expressing your interest in the position and highlighting your qualifications for the role, and then asking if the company has a salary range or if they are open to discussing compensation. It's important to approach the conversation professionally and be prepared to back up your salary request with reasons why you believe you deserve a certain salary or benefits.

You should avoid speaking about the salary right away because it can create a negative impression that you are only interested in the job for the money. It is important to show your interest and passion for the job first and then move onto the salary discussion once you have established a positive rapport with the interviewer and they have expressed interest in hiring you. Additionally, if you start the salary negotiation too early, you may not have all the information you need to make an informed decision about the compensation package, such as the benefits and perks that come with the job. It is better to wait until you have a clearer picture of the entire package before negotiating the salary.

When considering a job offer, there are several elements of the package to take into account in order to determine whether it is complete or satisfying. Here are some key things to consider:

1. Salary: This is often the most important factor for many people. Consider whether the salary being offered is in line with your expectations, and whether it reflects the value you bring to the position.

2. Benefits: This includes things like health insurance, retirement plans, and paid time off. Make sure you understand what benefits are included in the package and whether they meet your needs.

3. Bonus and commission: If the position comes with the potential for bonuses or commission, be sure to understand how these are calculated and what the potential payout could be.

4. Stock options or equity: Some companies offer employees stock options or equity as part of their compensation package. If this is the case, be sure to understand the terms and conditions of the options, and what potential value they could offer.

5. Perks and other considerations: This can include things like flexible work arrangements, company-provided equipment or tools, and other perks like gym memberships or transportation benefits.

It's important to weigh all of these factors together when considering a job offer. A high salary may be attractive, but if the benefits or other elements of the package are not in line with your needs, it may not be the best fit for you. Similarly, a lower salary with strong benefits and other perks may be a better overall package.

It's essential to do your research before going into an interview or a salary negotiation. Researching the company and the position you are interviewing for can help you better understand the organization's values, culture, and goals.

This information can be used to tailor your responses to interview questions and show that you have a genuine interest in the position.

Additionally, researching industry standards for salaries and benefits can help you have a realistic expectation of what to ask for during the negotiation. It can also give you leverage in negotiating for better compensation and benefits if you have information that supports your request.

Overall, doing your research can help you avoid disappointment, demonstrate your interest and knowledge of the company and industry, and give you leverage during the negotiation process.

It's hard to say for certain whether the company will offer you the top end of their pay scale or not. However, if their pay scale for the same position is $60,000 to $80,000 and your offer is in the range of $65,000 to $75,000, it's unlikely that they will offer you the top end of their pay scale.

It's important to keep in mind that the company has a budget and needs to balance their expenses. They will offer a salary that is fair and reasonable based on the market value of the position, your experience and skills, and their budget. It's up to you to negotiate and try to get the best offer possible within the company's constraints.

If your range is significantly higher than the company's pay scale or industry standard, it may be more difficult to negotiate a higher salary. However, it's still important to communicate your value and negotiate for a salary that reflects your skills and experience. If the company is interested in hiring you, they may be willing to make adjustments to their budget or salary range to accommodate your qualifications. However, this is not always guaranteed and will depend on the company's budget and policies. It's important to have realistic expectations and to negotiate in a professional and respectful manner.

If you have inside information that the pay range for the position is 60-80k and your offer is 65-85k, it's possible that the company may be willing to negotiate with you to come to a mutually agreeable salary. However, it's important to keep in mind that every situation is unique and there are many factors that can influence the outcome of salary negotiations.

It's important to approach the negotiation with a clear understanding of your own worth and the value you bring to the company, as well as a realistic understanding of industry standards and the company's budget. You may also want to consider other factors beyond salary, such as benefits, work-life balance, and opportunities for growth and development. Ultimately, the goal is to arrive at a compensation package that is fair and equitable for both you and the company.

If they only offer the minimum of the range, it can be disappointing if you were hoping for a higher salary. However, it's important to keep in mind that negotiation is a process, and there may be room to negotiate for a higher salary or other benefits. It's important to consider the entire compensation package and not just the salary, and to be prepared to negotiate for what you feel is fair and reasonable.

If the salary offer is not as high as expected, you can also negotiate for other benefits such as additional vacation time, flexible work hours, stock options, or professional development opportunities. It's important to consider the overall value of the compensation package, not just the base salary. However, it's still important to have realistic expectations and not expect to receive a salary offer that is significantly above the industry or company standard.

It's important to prioritize which benefits are most important to you and be flexible in the negotiation process. Keep in mind that some benefits, such as additional vacation time or flexible work hours, may not have a direct financial value but can greatly improve your work-life balance and overall job satisfaction.

However, it's also important to have realistic expectations and not expect to receive a salary offer that is significantly above the industry or company standard. Doing your research beforehand and having a clear understanding of the salary range for your position and experience level can help you set realistic expectations and negotiate more effectively.

A disappointing compensation package can be a trigger for renegotiation. However, it's important to approach the conversation with a positive and professional attitude, and to have a clear understanding of what you are asking for and why. You should also have a solid justification for why you believe a renegotiation is necessary. This may include factors such as changes in the job responsibilities, increased performance or achievements, or changes in the market or industry that have affected compensation standards. It's important to be specific and provide evidence to support your arguments.

Renegotiation can be done under certain conditions, such as:

1. Meeting or exceeding performance expectations: If you've been working hard and exceeding expectations, you may be in a good position to renegotiate your compensation.
2. Change in job responsibilities: If your job duties have significantly increased or changed, you may be able to renegotiate your compensation to reflect the new responsibilities.
3. Change in company policy or market conditions: If the company has changed its policies regarding compensation or the market conditions have changed, you may be able to renegotiate your compensation.
4. Long-term employment: If you have been working with the company for a long time and have a good track record, you may be able to renegotiate your compensation.

It's important to approach the renegotiation conversation professionally and with a clear understanding of your worth and the company's expectations.

The conversation for negotiating renegotiation can be started by expressing your appreciation for the opportunity to work for the company and explaining that you are looking forward to contributing to the company's success. Then, you can mention that you would like to revisit your compensation after a certain period of time, such as six months or a year, to ensure that it is in line with your contributions and the market standards.

It's important to frame the conversation in a positive way and emphasize your commitment to the company's success. You can also mention any specific accomplishments or projects that you have completed that demonstrate your value to the company. This will help to show that you are a valuable asset to the company and deserving of a renegotiation in the future.

Negotiating a future renegotiation can be tricky, but it can be done by setting clear expectations and establishing a timeline for when the renegotiation will take place. Here are some steps you can take:

1. Be upfront about your expectations: During the negotiation, express your desire to revisit the compensation package in the future. Explain that you understand that the company's budget may not allow for a higher salary at this time, but you would like to revisit the topic once you have proven your value to the company.

2. Establish a timeline: Set a specific timeline for when the renegotiation will take place. This could be after a certain amount of time has passed, after you have completed a major project or achieved a specific goal, or after a certain period of time has elapsed (e.g. one year). Be sure to get agreement from the employer on the timeline.

3. Agree on metrics: In order to facilitate the future renegotiation, agree on specific metrics or goals that will be used to evaluate your performance. This will give you a clear benchmark to work towards and will help to objectively demonstrate your value to the company.

4. Follow up: As the renegotiation date approaches, be sure to follow up with your employer to remind them of the agreement and to set a specific date for the renegotiation meeting.

5. Prepare for the renegotiation: When the time comes to renegotiate, be prepared to make a strong case for why you deserve a higher salary. Use data and metrics to demonstrate your value to the company and be prepared to negotiate on other benefits as well, such as additional vacation time or professional development opportunities.

Renegotiation for entering a company for the first time is possible, but it may be more difficult than renegotiating an existing contract. It's important to negotiate your initial offer as best as possible before accepting the job. However, if you find out that you're not satisfied with your salary or benefits after starting the job, you can still have a conversation with your employer about renegotiation.

If you do decide to renegotiate your initial offer, it's important to have a clear understanding of why you deserve a higher salary or better benefits. This may include providing evidence of your qualifications, experience, and achievements, as well as demonstrating how your skills and contributions are valuable to the company. You can also research industry standards and comparable positions to support your case.

When initiating a renegotiation for an initial offer, it's important to approach the conversation professionally and respectfully. Schedule a meeting with your supervisor or HR representative and express your concerns in a calm and rational manner. It's also important to listen to their perspective and be open to compromise.

It's worth noting that renegotiation for an initial offer may not always be successful, and it's important to have a backup plan in case the company is unable to meet your requests.

Renegotiation when entering a company for the first time is usually done to ensure that you are being compensated fairly based on your skills, experience, and the industry standard. It may not necessarily be because you are overqualified, but rather because you believe that you deserve a higher salary or better benefits based on your qualifications and the value you bring to the company. It's important to do your research and have a clear understanding of your worth in the job market before entering into any negotiation discussions.

It's understandable to prioritize salary when considering a job offer, as it is an important factor in ensuring financial stability and security. However, it's also important to consider other factors such as job satisfaction, growth opportunities, and work-life balance.

Regarding the interviewer's statement about making adjustments in the future, it's important to approach it with a level of skepticism. While it's possible that the company may provide salary increases in the future, it's not a guarantee, and it's important to have a realistic expectation about the compensation package being offered.

If salary is a top priority, it's important to negotiate effectively during the initial job offer to ensure that you are being compensated fairly for your qualifications and experience. It's also important to have an open and honest conversation with the interviewer about your expectations and needs in terms of compensation.

Other means of remuneration refer to non-cash compensation or benefits that an employee can receive in addition to their salary. These benefits can include:

1. Health insurance: Many companies offer health insurance benefits to their employees as part of their compensation package. This can include medical, dental, and vision insurance.
2. Retirement plans: Employers may offer retirement plans such as a 401(k) or pension plan to help employees save for their future.
3. Stock options: Some companies may offer stock options to their employees, which allow them to purchase company stock at a

discounted rate.

4.	Bonuses: Bonuses are usually given to employees as a reward for achieving specific goals or milestones.
5.	Paid time off: Paid time off (PTO) can include vacation days, sick leave, and personal days.
6.	Flexible work arrangements: Some companies may offer flexible work arrangements such as telecommuting, flexible hours, or a compressed workweek.
7.	Tuition reimbursement: Tuition reimbursement programs can help employees pay for education and training programs that can enhance their skills and knowledge.
8.	Company perks: Companies may offer other perks such as gym memberships, free snacks or drinks, or company events.

It's important to consider these other means of remuneration when evaluating a job offer or negotiating your compensation package. Sometimes, the value of these benefits can outweigh a higher salary offer.

Ultimately, the decision to accept or decline a job offer is up to the individual and their personal circumstances. It's important to carefully consider the entire compensation package, including salary, benefits, and any potential growth or advancement opportunities, before making a decision. If the offer does not meet your expectations, you may choose to negotiate or decline the offer and continue your job search.

Recap

Here's a recap of some of the key points we discussed:

1. Research the company and the industry before the interview. This will help you to understand the company's culture, values, and mission, and to demonstrate your knowledge and interest in the company during the interview.
2. Practice your interview skills, including your answers to common interview questions and your body language. This will help you to feel more confident and prepared during the interview.
3. Dress appropriately and choose a quiet, distraction-free environment for a virtual interview.
4. Avoid speaking about salary right away during the interview. Instead, focus on demonstrating your skills, experience, and qualifications.
5. If the interviewer asks for a specific number, be prepared with a range based on your research and market value. However, try to avoid giving a specific number if possible.
6. Consider negotiating for other benefits if the salary offer is not as high as expected. These may include additional vacation time, flexible work hours, stock options, or professional development opportunities.
7. It's important to have realistic expectations and not expect to receive a salary offer that is significantly above the industry or company standard.
8. If the initial salary offer is disappointing, you can try to negotiate for a higher salary or other benefits, but be prepared to walk away if the company is not willing to meet your expectations.
9. Other means of remuneration may include bonuses, commissions, profit sharing, or other types of incentives.
10. Finally, applying to companies you don't necessarily want to work for can be a good way to practice your interview skills, learn more about the industry, and potentially discover new opportunities.

Understanding non-verbal signals is an essential skill in communication, especially in job interviews and salary negotiations. Non-verbal communication can reveal a person's attitude, emotions, and intentions, and being able to read and interpret these signals can help you understand the interviewer's perspective and respond appropriately.

The science of non-verbal signals is based on the idea that our body language, facial expressions, and tone of voice convey information that complements or contradicts our verbal messages. For example, if an interviewer says, "We're really interested in your qualifications," but their arms are crossed and their face looks bored, the non-verbal signals suggest they may not be as enthusiastic as their words imply.

Some common non-verbal signals to watch for include:

- Eye contact: Maintaining steady eye contact conveys confidence and sincerity, while avoiding eye contact may indicate discomfort or dishonesty.
- Facial expressions: Smiling, nodding, and raised eyebrows indicate agreement and interest, while frowning or pursed lips suggest disagreement or disapproval.
- Posture: Sitting up straight and leaning forward shows engagement and interest, while slouching or leaning back can indicate boredom or disinterest.
- Gestures: Hand movements and body language can reveal enthusiasm, nervousness, or irritation, depending on the context.
- Tone of voice: The pitch, volume, and speed of speech can convey emotions such as enthusiasm, nervousness, or frustration.

In order to interpret non-verbal signals accurately, it's important to look for patterns and context. A single gesture or expression may not tell the whole story, but a combination of signals over time can give you a better sense of the interviewer's attitudes and intentions. It's also important to be aware of your own non-verbal signals and how they may be perceived by the interviewer. For example, fidgeting or avoiding eye contact may convey nervousness or lack of confidence, while open and engaged body language can convey confidence and interest.

In addition to interpreting non-verbal signals, you can also use non-verbal communication to your advantage in job interviews and salary negotiations. For example, maintaining eye contact, smiling, and sitting up straight can convey confidence and engagement. Mirroring the interviewer's gestures and posture can also create a sense of rapport and connection.

Overall, understanding the science of non-verbal signals can help you navigate job interviews and salary negotiations with greater confidence and success. By paying attention to both your own non-verbal signals and those of the interviewer, you can communicate effectively and build rapport, leading to more positive outcomes.

Developing a winner's mindset and becoming more confident in your abilities is a key component to succeeding in any aspect of life, including job interviews and salary negotiations. Here are some tips on how to develop a winner's mindset and boost your confidence:

1. Believe in Yourself: One of the most important aspects of developing a winner's mindset is believing in yourself and your abilities. Confidence comes from within, and if you don't believe in yourself, it will be difficult to convince others to believe in you. Take time to reflect on your past achievements and successes, and use those experiences to fuel your self-belief.

2. Embrace Failure: Failure is a natural part of the learning process, and it's important to embrace it as an opportunity for growth and improvement. Rather than getting discouraged by setbacks or rejections, use them as learning experiences and opportunities to refine your approach.

3. Practice Mindfulness: Mindfulness is the practice of being present in the moment and fully engaged in your surroundings. By practicing mindfulness, you can better manage your emotions and reduce anxiety and stress, which can help you feel more confident in your abilities.

4. Visualize Success: Visualization is a powerful technique that can help you create a mental image of success. Take time to visualize yourself succeeding in the job interview and salary negotiation process. Imagine yourself confidently answering questions and making

compelling arguments for your desired salary range.

5. Surround Yourself with Positive Influences: Surrounding yourself with positive influences, such as supportive friends and family members, can help boost your confidence and provide a strong support system. Seek out mentors or role models who can offer guidance and support.

6. Prepare Thoroughly: Preparation is key to feeling confident in any situation. Take time to research the company, the job role, and the salary range for similar positions. Practice answering common interview questions and develop a strategy for negotiating your desired salary range.

By developing a winner's mindset and boosting your confidence, you can approach job interviews and salary negotiations with a sense of calm and self-assurance. Remember to believe in yourself, embrace failure as an opportunity for growth, practice mindfulness, visualize success, surround yourself with positive influences, and prepare thoroughly for the interview and salary negotiation process.

Preparing for an interview is key to success. Make sure you are well prepared and know what to do right before your interview.

Making a great first impression is crucial in any job interview. Make sure to have a positive first impression. Remember that making a great first impression is just the beginning. You will also need to back up your initial impression with your qualifications, experience, and ability to answer questions effectively.

Handling challenging questions during an interview can be nerve-wracking, but it is an essential skill to master in order to make a good impression on the interviewer. Show your thought process, when answering a challenging question; it's often helpful to show your thought process. Talk through how you arrived at your answer, even if it's not the correct one. This can demonstrate your critical thinking skills and problem-solving abilities.

Handling virtual interviews is becoming increasingly common in today's job market, make a positive impression and have a successful virtual interview.

Negotiating your salary can be an intimidating process, but it is an important step in ensuring that you are fairly compensated for your work. Remember, negotiating your salary is a normal part of the job search process, and it's important to advocate for yourself and your worth. With preparation and confidence, you can successfully negotiate a salary that reflects your value and experience.

Wishing you every happiness and success in your new position.

Did you love *Nailing the Interview: Tips and Techniques for Crushing Your Next Interview*? Then you should read *Going up: The Art of Salary Negotiation*[1] by AF Delk!

[2]

Salary negotiation can be a nerve-wracking experience for many individuals, especially if they are not familiar with the process or lack the necessary negotiation skills. However, it is a crucial skill to possess in today's job market, as it can significantly impact your earnings and career trajectory. This is where the book "Going Up: The Art of Salary Negotiation" by AF Delk comes in - to provide readers with powerful strategies and tactics for effective salary negotiation. One of the key insights from this book is that negotiation is not just about the words that you say, but about the relationships that you build with the people you are negotiating with. This chapter provides readers with guidance on how to build strong relationships with employers, even before the negotiation begins. It also explores the psychology of negotiation, and how understanding the motivations and concerns of the other party can help

---

1. https://books2read.com/u/31Q2zD

2. https://books2read.com/u/31Q2zD

you to negotiate more effectively."Going Up: The Art of Salary Negotiation" is its practical approach to negotiation. The book provides clear examples of negotiation scenarios and offers step-by-step guidance on how to approach each situation. This makes it easy for readers to apply the concepts they learn in the book to real-world situations."Going Up: The Art of Salary Negotiation" emphasizes building relationships with employers. The book explains that negotiation is not a one-time event, but an ongoing process that involves building trust and credibility with your employer. It provides practical tips on how to establish rapport with your employer and develop a long-term relationship based on mutual respect and trust.The book also includes a chapter on the psychology of negotiation, which is an essential aspect of effective negotiation. It explains how to understand and leverage the psychological factors that influence negotiation outcomes, such as emotions, biases, and power dynamics. This knowledge can help readers develop a more effective negotiation style and achieve better outcomes in their negotiations.One of the unique features of "Going Up: The Art of Salary Negotiation" is its focus on the ethical dimensions of negotiation. The book emphasizes the importance of ethical behavior in negotiation and provides practical guidance on how to negotiate in an ethical and responsible manner. It also discusses the potential ethical dilemmas that can arise in negotiation and offers strategies for handling them.The final chapter of the book is dedicated to the art of closing the deal. It provides practical advice on how to make a final decision, accept or decline an offer, and negotiate the final details of the agreement. The book emphasizes the importance of being clear, concise, and respectful in your communication with the employer during the closing phase of negotiation.Overall, "Going Up: The Art of Salary Negotiation" is a comprehensive and practical guide to effective salary negotiation. It provides readers with powerful strategies and tactics for negotiation, as well as practical guidance on how to apply these concepts in real-world situations. The book is suitable for individuals at any stage of their career, from entry-level positions to senior management roles.Whether you're a recent college graduate or a seasoned professional, this book can help you achieve your desired salary and take your career to the next level. It is a must-read for anyone who wants to improve their negotiation skills and increase their earning potential. So, if you want to go up in your career and negotiate your way to success, get your hands on "Going Up: The Art of Salary Negotiation" today!

About the Author

Despite facing challenges from dyslexia and ADHD, he developed a remarkable resilience that became the foundation for his many successes. His unique perspective and drive allowed him to become a certified mechanical engineer and rise to the top of multiple companies in a short period. However, he quickly realized that his success was coming at a cost to his family life. Rather than compromise on what matters most, he made the courageous decision to retire from his high-flying career in his early thirties and become a full-time freelancer. This bold move allowed him to spend more quality time with his family, and his freelance work still allowed him to showcase his skills in a way that is flexible and balanced. He is now able to be present and supportive of his beloved children and never misses a moment of their lives. His experience and dedication make him an invaluable member of any team, and he has proven that even with adversity, great success can be achieved.